MCRP 3-11.2A

Marine Troop Leader's Guide

U.S. Marine Corps

PCN 144 000121 00

DEPARTMENT OF THE NAVY
Headquarters United States Marine Corps
Washington, DC 20380-1775

16 March 1995

FOREWORD

1. PURPOSE

Fleet Marine Force Reference Publication (FMFRP) 0-6, *Marine Troop Leader's Guide*, provides a checklist of basic duties for the troop leader at the platoon, section, squad, and fire team levels in combat operations.

2. SCOPE

This FMFRP includes the specific duties of troop leaders in the amphibious and helicopterborne assault, offensive and defensive operations ashore, selected operations other than war, and special types of land operations. Specific information concerning the tactics and techniques applicable to the employment of these units is contained in FMFM 6-4, *Marine Rifle Company/Platoon* and FMFM 6-5, *Marine Rifle Squad*. This publication is designed for use as a field reference guide.

3. SUPERSESSION

FMFM 1-2, *Marine Troop Leader's Guide* dated 5 April 1979.

4. CHANGES

Recommendations for improving this manual are invited from commands as well as directly from individuals. Forward suggestions using the User Suggestion Form format to —

>Commanding General
>Doctrine Division (C 42)
>Marine Corps Combat Development Command
>2042 Broadway Street, Suite 210
>Quantico, Virginia 22134-5021

5. CERTIFICATION

Reviewed and approved this date.

BY DIRECTION OF THE
COMMANDANT OF THE MARINE CORPS

C. E. WILHELM
Lieutenant General, U.S. Marine Corps
Commanding General
Marine Corps Combat Development Command
Quantico, Virginia

DISTRIBUTION: 140 000060 00

User Suggestion Form

From:

To: Commanding General
     Doctrine Division (C 42)
     Marine Corps Combat Development Command
     2042 Broadway Street Suite 210
     Quantico, Virginia 22134-5021

Subj: RECOMMENDATIONS CONCERNING FMFRP 0-6, *MARINE TROOP LEADER'S GUIDE*

1. In accordance with the foreword to FMFRP 0-6, which invites individuals to submit suggestions concerning this FMFRP directly to the above addressee, the following unclassified recommendation is forwarded:

___   _____   _____   _____
Page   Article/Paragraph No.   Line No.   Figure/Table No.

Nature of Change: ☐ Add
                     ☐ Delete
                     ☐ Change
                     ☐ Correct

2. Proposed new verbatim text: (Verbatim, double-spaced; continue on additional pages as necessary.)

3. Justification/source: (Need not be double-spaced.)

NOTE: Only one recommendation per page.

Record of Changes

MARINE TROOP LEADER'S GUIDE

TABLE OF CONTENTS

Chapter 1   Rifle Platoon

General Duties 1-1
   Rifle Platoon Commander 1-1
   Rifle Platoon Sergeant 1-2

Amphibious Operations 1-3
   Pre-embarkation Duties 1-3
   Duties Aboard Ship 1-5
   Duties During Ship-to-Shore Movement 1-7
   Duties During Assault 1-8

Helicopterborne Operations 1-9
   Training Duties 1-9
   Planning Duties 1-10
   Duties in the Assembly Area 1-11
   Duties During Initial Ground Action 1-12

Offensive Combat 1-12
   Movement to Contact — Foot March 1-13
   Movement to Contact — Motorized March 1-19
   Duties in the Assembly Area 1-20
   Daylight Attack 1-21
   Night Attack 1-28
   Mechanized Infantry Attack 1-33
   Infantry/Tank Attacks 1-35
   Attack of Fortified Areas 1-37
   Attack of Urban Terrain 1-39
   River-Crossing Operations 1-41

Defensive Combat 1-44
   Frontline Platoon 1-44
   Reserve Platoon, Frontline Company 1-53
   Reverse Slope Defense 1-55
   Platoon as a Security Force 1-56
   Defense of Urban Terrain 1-58

Relief Operations 1-59
   Relief in Place 1-60
   Passage of Lines 1-63

Retrograde Operations 1-65
   Night Withdrawal 1-65
   Daylight Withdrawal 1-66
   Delaying Action 1-68

Mine Warfare 1-69
   Conventional Minefield Installation 1-69
   Minefield Breaching 1-76

Mob and Riot Control 1-76

Noncombatant Evacuation Operations 1-79
   Training 1-79
   Planning and Conduct of the Mission 1-80

Humanitarian Assistance/Disaster Relief 1-81
   Training 1-81
   Planning and Conduct of the Mission 1-82

Chapter 2   Rifle Squad

General Duties 2-1

Amphibious Operations. 2-2
    Pre-embarkation Duties 2-2
    Duties Aboard Ship 2-3
    Duties During Ship-to-Shore Movement 2-4
    Duties During Assault 2-6

Helicopterborne Operations 2-7
    Training Duties 2-7
    Planning Duties 2-7
    Duties in the Assembly Area 2-8
    Duties During Initial Ground Action 2-9

Offensive Combat 2-9
    Movement to Contact — Foot March 2-9
    Movement to Contact — Mechanized March 2-14
    Duties in the Assembly Area 2-14
    Daylight Attack 2-15
    Night Attack 2-20
    Mechanized Infantry Attack 2-22
    Attack of Fortified Areas 2-23
    Attack of Urban Terrain 2-26
    River-Crossing Operations 2-27

Defensive Combat 2-28
    Squad of Frontline Platoon 2-28
    Squad in the Security Area 2-34
    Squad in the Defense of Urban Terrain 2-35

Relief Operations 2-36
    Relief in Place 2-37
    Passage of Lines 2-38

Retrograde Operations 2-39
    Night Withdrawal 2-40
    Daylight Withdrawal 2-42
    Delaying Action 2-42

Mine Warfare 2-43
    Hasty Protective Minefield Installation 2-43
    Minefield Breaching 2-44

Mob and Riot Control 2-44

Chapter 3 Fire Team

General Duties 3-1

Amphibious Operations 3-2
    Pre-embarkation Duties 3-2
    Duties Aboard Ship 3-2
    Duties During Ship-to-Shore Movement 3-3
    Duties During Assault 3-3

Helicopterborne Operations 3-4
    Training Duties 3-4
    Duties in the Assembly and Holding Areas 3-5
    Duties During Initial Ground Action 3-5

Offensive Combat 3-6
    Movement to Contact 3-6
    Duties in the Assembly Area 3-8
    Daylight Attack 3-9
    Night Attack 3-12
    Mechanized Infantry Attack 3-14
    Attack of Fortified Areas 3-15
    Attack of Urban Terrain 3-16
    River-Crossing Operations 3-18

Defensive Combat 3-18
  Fire Team of Frontline Squad 3-18
  Fire Team as Part of a Security Element 3-22
  Fire Team in the Defense of Urban Terrain 3-22

Relief Operations 3-23
  Relief in Place 3-23
  Passage of Lines 3-24

Retrograde Operations 3-24
  Night Withdrawal 3-25
  Daylight Withdrawal 3-26
  Delaying Action 3-27

Mob and Riot Control 3-28

Chapter 4   Weapons Platoon— Platoon Commander

General Duties 4-1
  Weapons Platoon Commander 4-1
  Weapons Platoon Sergeant 4-3

Amphibious Operations 4-3
  Pre-embarkation Duties 4-3
  Duties Aboard Ship 4-5
  Duties During Ship-to-Shore Movement 4-7
  Duties During Assault 4-7

Helicopterborne Operations 4-8
  Training Duties 4-8
  Planning Duties 4-9
  Duties in the Assembly Area 4-10
  Duties During Initial Ground Action 4-10

Offensive Combat 4-10
    Movement to Contact — Foot March 4-11
    Movement to Contact — Motorized March 4-11
    Duties in the Assembly Area 4-12
    Daylight Attack 4-14
    Night Attack 4-20
    Other Offensive Operations 4-22

Defensive Combat 4-25
    Weapons Platoon in the Defense 4-25
    Weapons Platoon in the Defense of Urban Terrain 4-31

Relief Operations 4-31
    Relief in Place 4-32
    Passage of Lines 4-34

Retrograde Operations 4-35
    Withdrawal and Delaying Action 4-35

Mob and Riot Control 4-36

Chapter 5   Weapons Platoon — Section Leader

General Duties 5-1

Amphibious Operations 5-2
    Pre-embarkation Duties 5-2
    Duties Aboard Ship 5-3
    Duties During Ship-to-Shore Movement 5-4
    Duties During Assault 5-4

Helicopterborne Operations 5-4
   Training Duties 5-4
   Planning Duties 5-5
   Duties in the Assembly Area 5-6
   Duties During Initial Ground Action 5-6

Offensive Combat 5-7
   Movement to Contact — Foot March 5-7
   Movement to Contact — Motorized March 5-8
   Duties in the Assembly Area 5-8
   Daylight Attack 5-9
   Night Attack 5-15
   Other Offensive Operations 5-17

Defensive Combat 5-19
   Section in the Defense 5-19
   Section in the Defense of Urban Terrain 5-23

Relief Operations 5-23
   Relief in Place 5-24
   Passage of Lines 5-25

Retrograde Operations 5-26
   Withdrawal and Delaying Action 5-26

Chapter 6 Weapons Platoon —Squad Leader

General Duties 6-1

Amphibious Operations 6-2
   Pre-embarkation Duties 6-2
   Duties Aboard Ship 6-3
   Duties During Ship-to-Shore Movement 6-3
   Duties During Assault 6-4

Helicopterborne Operations 6-5
    Training Duties 6-5
    Duties in the Assembly Area 6-6
    Duties During Initial Ground Action 6-6

Offensive Combat 6-7
    Movement to Contact — Foot March 6-7
    Movement to Contact — Motorized March 6-7
    Duties in the Assembly Area 6-8
    Daylight Attack 6-9
    Night Attack 6-13
    Other Offensive Operations 6-14

Defensive Combat 6-17
    Squad in the Defense 6-17
    Squad in the Defense of Urban Terrain 6-20

Relief Operations 6-21
    Relief in Place 6-21
    Passage of Lines 6-23

Retrograde Operations 6-23
    Withdrawal 6-23
    Delaying Action 6-24

Appendixes

A	Troop Leading Procedures.	A-1
B	Duties of the Boat Team and Assistant Boat Team Commanders	B-1
C	Helicopterborne Operations.	C-1
D	Intelligence Procedures	D-1
E	Duties of the Patrol Leader	E-1
F	Fire Support Requests	F-1
G	Duties of Leaders for NBC Defense.	G-1
H	Tactical Bivouacs	H-1
I	Arm and Hand Signals.	I-1
J	Glossary	J-1

CHAPTER 1

RIFLE PLATOON

The **mission** of the **rifle platoon** is to locate, close with, and destroy the enemy by fire and maneuver, or to repel the enemy's assault by fire and close combat.

This chapter discusses the duties of the rifle platoon **commander**

General Duties

In addition to the procedures prescribed for all troop leaders in appendix A, the rifle platoon commander will —

- Plan and conduct the tactical training of the rifle platoon in accordance with company training directives.

- Direct and control the tactical employment of the rifle platoon in combat and training operations through the use of appropriate troop leading procedures.

- Prepare and revise estimates of the situation continually during the conduct of operations in order to more effectively accomplish assigned tactical missions.

- Coordinate the employment of the rifle platoon with adjacent units and, as appropriate, with units supporting the platoon mission.

- Ensure the timely requisition, distribution, safeguarding, and economical use of supplies and equipment.

- Ensure first echelon maintenance of weapons and equipment through frequent inspections.

- Supervise the administrative functions of the platoon, including records relating to personnel, training, and combat casualties.

- Enhance combat efficiency, discipline, and morale by the application of standard health, comfort, and welfare measures consistent with tactical considerations.

The rifle platoon commander is assisted in his duties by the rifle **platoon sergeant** who will —

- Perform those duties assigned by the platoon commander.
- Assume command in the absence of the platoon commander.
- Assist in all aspects of supervision and control of the platoon.
- Perform those administrative and logistics functions directed by the platoon commander.
- Be directly responsible to the platoon commander for the supply and timely resupply of the platoon in combat.
- Maintain a casualty record and coordinate the medical evacuation of casualties.

Amphibious Operations

In addition to the general duties prescribed on page 1-1, the platoon commander is responsible for performing the following actions during amphibious operations.

PRE-EMBARKATION DUTIES

The rifle platoon commander will —

- Conduct training in platoon tactics, independent squad action, development of small unit leadership skills, and techniques of the ship-to-shore movement:
  - Supervise instruction for the individual in —
    - Ground combat skills.
    - Rigging of individual weapons, equipment, and life preservers for debarkation.
    - Lashing techniques for crew-served weapons and equipment.
    - Debarkation procedures.
    - Actions aboard ship, landing craft, assault amphibious vehicle (AAV), and aircraft.
    - Procedures for emergency abandonment of AAVs and/or landing craft.

  - Direct and control training for the unit in —
    - Small-unit tactics.
    - The basic procedures and control involved in the ship-to-shore movement.
    - Naval customs and troop life aboard ship.

RIFLE PLATOON — Amphibious Ops

- Select key members of the boat teams and conduct training in the purpose, functioning, and organization of the boat team. Emphase the duties and responsibilities of the boat team commander, assistant boat team commander, coxswains, and the deck and boat loaders.

■ Prepare a plan:
- Make a detailed study of available planning aids. These include maps, aerial and shoreline photographs, area and objective studies, intelligence reports, and summaries.
- Make a preliminary estimate of the situation.
- Formulate a tentative plan of attack to include employment of squads, scheme of maneuver, initial formations, and supporting fires.
- Submit tentative plan of attack to the company commander.
- Submit platoon landing craft, helicopter, or assault amphibious vehicle assignments to the company commander. Organize boat teams based on —
  - Plan of attack.
  - Composition of the unit.
  - Type and number of landing craft or amphibious vehicles assigned.
  - Tactical integrity of subordinate units.
  - Dispersion of crew-served weapons and key personnel.
- Conduct familiarization firing and set battle sights.
- Ensure preparedness of weapons, clothing, and equipment for the operation.

- Check service records to verify that the data contained therein is current and correct as indicated in the following:
    - Record of Emergency Data (RED).
    - Eligibility for combat.
    - ID/Geneva Convention Cards (DD2MC).
    - Serviceman's Group Life Insurance.
    - Wills.
    - Powers of Attorney.

- Take steps to obtain essential special equipment prior to embarkation, including boat paddles and lashing lines.

- Ensure complete preparedness for embarkation, as directed.

DUTIES ABOARD SHIP

The rifle platoon commander will —

- Inspect the platoon berthing space.
- Determine the adequacy and serviceability of —
    - Bunks and linens.
    - Life preservers.
    - Lockers.
    - Heads.
    - Weapons storage areas.
    - Common personal effects storage lockers.
    - Dining facilities and food quality.

- Laundry service.

■ Assign bunks to subordinate units by blocks in order to facilitate rapid debarkation

■ Brief the platoon concerning —

- Actions to be taken during ship drills.
- Applicable ship regulations.
- Musters.
- Messing.
- Use of ship's facilities, to include the barber shop, library, movies, ship store, and laundry.
- Assignments to ship's platoon.

■ Inspect the following daily and correct or report deficiencies:

- Personnel.
- Weapons and equipment for serviceability and maintenance.
- Troop compartment to ensure —
  - Decks and bulkheads are clean.
  - Head facilities and scuttlebutts are clean and operable.
  - Bunks are made and properly secured.
  - Equipment is properly stowed and secured.
  - Weapons are secure.
  - Ventilation systems are functioning and unobstructed.
  - Ship's equipment is properly maintained.

■ Conduct and supervise training to include —

- Physical conditioning exercises.

- Military subjects, stressing those which are important to the operation.
- Maintenance of weapons and equipment.

■ Conduct operational planning:

- Brief the platoon on the company mission, rehearsal schedule, debarkation procedures and serial assignments, and the ship-to-shore movement plan.
- Complete a tentative plan.

■ Issue the order and ensure thorough understanding by utilizing mockups, sketches, maps, aerial photographs, and question and answer techniques.

■ Conduct a final check of newly joined or accompanying personnel to ensure identification data is properly recorded for casualty reporting.

■ Ensure that each person has been assimilated into the team.

DUTIES DURING SHIP-TO-SHORE MOVEMENT

The rifle platoon commander will —

■ Supervise the boat teams in assembly and preparation for debarkation.

■ Carry out the duties of boat team commander, as described in appendix B.

■ Keep the company commander informed of the situation, consistent with communications instructions.

- Review with available subordinate unit leaders the details of such items as the landing beach and surrounding terrain.
- Consider the following for small boat landings:
  - Location, type, and range of enemy sensors, alarms, or radar.
  - Patrols near the beach landing site.
  - Schedules and routes of patrol craft.
  - Schedules and capabilities of air patrols.
  - Wire, mines, or lights near the beach landing site.
  - Alert status of units near the beach landing site.
  - Offshore platforms and anchorages that may interfere with the route.
  - Capability to reinforce the area of the beach landing site.
  - Proper cache of craft as required.

DUTIES DURING ASSAULT

The rifle platoon commander will —

- Establish tactical control of subordinate units ashore.
- Continue estimates of the situation.
- Revise current plans or develop new plans based on the current estimate of the situation.
- Inform the company commander of platoon location, situation, planned action, and all bypassed enemy positions.

Helicopterborne Operations

In addition to the general duties prescribed on page 1-1, the rifle platoon commander is responsible for performing the following actions during helicopterborne operations.

TRAINING DUTIES

The rifle platoon commander will —

- Conduct individual training in —
  - Embarkation and debarkation procedures.
  - Conduct in flight.
  - Preparation of manifest tags.
  - Safety precautions.
  - Emergency procedures.
  - Use of emergency equipment.
  - Use of helicopter rope suspension training (HRST) equipment such as rapelling equipment, special patrol insertion and extraction (SPIE) rig, and Jacobs ladder.
  - Cable hoist procedures.
- Conduct platoon training in —
  - Heliteam organization and the duties of leaders (see appendix C).

- Actions in the assembly and holding areas, pickup zone, loading point, and landing site/zone.
- Initial ground orientation to include use of compass azimuth and terrain features.

■ Conduct drills related to —
- Initial ground action and readily identifiable terrain features.
- Reestablishment of tactical control.
- Use of compass azimuth for orientation.
- Safety procedures during emergency landing.

PLANNING DUTIES

The rifle platoon commander will —

■ Make a preliminary estimate of the situation.

■ Conduct map and/or aerial photograph reconnaissance.

■ Coordinate with the weapons platoon commander and the adjacent rifle platoon commander.

■ Formulate tentative plan of attack to include —
- Landing plan and heliteam organization.
- Scheme of maneuver.
    - Clearing all or a portion of the landing site.
    - Initial movement from the landing site.
    - Seizure of objectives.
- Fire support.

- Fires during helicopterborne movement.
- Fires in support of helicopterborne landing.
- Fires in support of the ground tactical plan.
- Use of naval surface fire support.
- Use of artillery.
- Use of mortars.
- Use of attack helicopters and fixed-wing aircraft.

■ Submit a tentative plan of attack and fire support request to the company commander.

■ Designate heliteam and assistant heliteam leaders.

■ Submit platoon heliteam wave and serial assignments based on —

- Plan of attack.
- Composition of unit.
- Type and number of helicopters assigned.
- Tactical integrity of subordinate units.
- Dispersion of crew-served weapons and key personnel.

■ Complete the plan and issue the order.

DUTIES IN THE ASSEMBLY AREA

The rifle platoon commander will —

■ Assemble the platoon and ensure that it is properly equipped.

RIFLE PLATOON — Offensive Combat

- Form the platoon into heliteams.
- Conduct a final briefing and orientation for the heliteam leaders.
- Ensure correct preparation of manifest tags.
- Conduct a final inspection of Marines and equipment.
- Carry out the duties of the heliteam leader for the helicopter in which embarked.

DUTIES DURING INITIAL GROUND ACTION

The rifle platoon commander will —

- Establish tactical control of the platoon.
- Continue estimates of the situation.
- Revise current plans or develop new plans based upon the estimate of the situation.
- Carry out the assigned mission.
- Maintain contact with the company commander.

Offensive Combat

In addition to the general duties prescribed on page 1-1, the rifle platoon commander is responsible for performing the following actions during offensive combat.

MOVEMENT TO CONTACT — FOOT MARCH

Platoon as Advance Party

The rifle platoon commander will —

- Conduct map and aerial photograph reconnaissance of the march route, to include obtaining updated information from current intelligence reports, with emphasis on —
  - Start, release, and checkpoints.
  - Critical points such as bridges, crossroads, tunnels, fords, or likely ambush sites.
- Include the following specific details in the march order:
  - Designation of a point squad.
  - Designation of flank security consistent with terrain.
  - Assignment of a sector of observation to each squad.
  - Designation of connecting files.
  - Location and employment of attached units.
  - Formation of an advance party.
  - March distances to be maintained between elements and individuals.
  - Route control features and rate of march.
  - Security measures during halts.
  - Assignment of air sentinels when dictated by the tactical situation.

- Take a position within the advance party from which the units making up the advance party can best be controlled. As the situation develops and the enemy is located, move to where the action can best be controlled and influenced.

- Follow the assigned route at the prescribed rate of march and report the platoon's arrival at control features.

- Report all enemy sighted.

- Engage the enemy in order to —
  - Destroy him.
  - Fix him by fire to cover the deployment of the support.
  - Clear the route and ensure the unimpeded advance of the main body.

- Report contact with the enemy including action taken, enemy location, disposition, and strength.

- Establish a defensive posture during halts.

Platoon as Flank Guard

The rifle platoon commander will —

- Conduct map and aerial photograph reconnaissance of the march route, to include obtaining updated information from current intelligence reports, with emphasis on —
  - Avenues of approach to the march route.
  - Key terrain features dominating avenues of approach to the march route.

- The influence of terrain on selection of flank squad formations.

■ Include the following specific details in the march order:

- Unit security measures.
- Assignment of a sector of observation to each squad.
- Location and employment of attached weapons.
- Tentative blocking positions.
- Initial formation.
- March distances between flank guard elements.
- Flank guard route and rate of march.
- Assignment of air sentinels when dictated by the tactical situation.

■ Select and clear key terrain features dominating avenues of approach to march column.

■ Search other areas likely to conceal the enemy or provide him with good observation of the march column.

■ Report all enemy sighted.

■ Engage the enemy in order to prevent exposure of the march column and protect the flank guard.

■ Report contact with the enemy including action taken, enemy location, disposition, and strength.

■ Resist enemy attack until ordered to withdraw.

- Take a position within the flank guard from which the unit composing the flank guard can best be controlled. As the situation develops and the enemy is located, move to where the action can best be controlled and influenced.

Platoon as Rear Guard

The rifle platoon commander will —

- Conduct map and aerial photograph reconnaissance of the march route, to include obtaining updated information from current intelligence reports, with emphasis on terrain which permits delaying actions.

- Include the following specific details in the march order:
  - Designation of a squad as rear point.
  - Designation of flank security consistent with terrain.
  - Assignment of a sector of observation for each squad.
  - Designation of connecting files.
  - Location and employment of attached units.
  - Employment of obstacles.
  - Formation of rear party.
  - March distances to be maintained between elements and individuals.
  - Route and rate of march.
  - Security measures.

- Assignment of air sentinels when dictated by the tactical situation.
- Make maximum use of obstacles.
- Select and utilize successive delaying positions.
- Report all enemy sighted.
- Conduct delaying actions.
- Report contact with the enemy including actions taken and enemy location, disposition, and strength.
- Report passage of all control features.

Platoon in Blocking Positions

Security elements previously discussed establish a defensive posture during halts of the march column. A blocking position may also be established by a unit from the main body assigned that mission. In establishing a blocking position, the rifle platoon commander will —

- Conduct map and aerial photograph reconnaissance, to include obtaining updated information from current intelligence reports, with emphasis on terrain that affords observation and fields of fire.
- Select outpost positions which prevent an enemy approach within small arms range of the march column.
- Include the following specific details in the march order:
  - Assignment of a position and route of withdrawal for each squad.
  - Designation of sectors of observation.

- Designation of fields of fire.
- Provision for continuous observation of avenues of approach.
- Location and employment of attached weapons.
- Provision for all-round security to include air sentinels.

■ Report all enemy sighted.

■ Engage the enemy, as necessary, and report action taken, enemy location, disposition, and strength.

■ Withdraw on order.

Platoon as Part of Support or Main Body

The rifle platoon commander will —

■ Conduct map and aerial photograph reconnaissance of the march route, to include obtaining updated information from current intelligence reports, with emphasis on all critical points.

■ Include the following specific details in the march order:
- Assignment of a sector of ground observation for each squad.
- Assignment of air sentinels.
- Designation of connecting files.
- Formation of support or main body.
- March distances to be maintained between units and individuals.
- Route and rate of march.
- Security measures during halts.

- Maintain march discipline.
- Ensure dispersion, unit security, and camouflage measures during halts.
- Prepare to assume other missions.

MOVEMENT TO CONTACT — MOTORIZED MARCH

In addition to the duties described in the previous section concerning foot marches, the following considerations apply to missions assigned for a motorized march.

The rifle platoon commander will —

- Ensure that wheeled vehicles are properly hardened.
- Establish additional radio communications.
- Provide for tactical integrity in vehicle assignments.
- Dispatch the point in terms of time intervals rather than distance.
- Ensure that the point and rear point vehicles conduct their advance by bounds or by alternate bounds.
- Provide for unit security ensuring mutual support by fire and observation, to include air sentinels.
- Move vehicles off roads and utilize available cover and concealment during halts.
- Ensure that troops are properly trained and rehearsed in immediate action drills for motorized marches.

RIFLE PLATOON — Offensive Combat

DUTIES IN THE ASSEMBLY AREA

The rifle platoon commander will —

- Assign areas to squads to provide for dispersion, unit security, and concealment.
- Issue a warning order to include —
  - Time of attack.
  - Platoon mission, company mission, battalion mission, and the intent of each commander.
  - Time and place for issuance of the combat order and scheduled rehearsals.
  - Administrative preparation for the attack.
- Take action to prepare or improve available cover.
- Exercise continuous camouflage and other counterintelligence measures against ground and air observation to include —
  - Removal of excess soil from positions.
  - Proper use and timely replacement of natural camouflage material.
  - Movement control measures to avoid creating visible paths.
  - Disposal of trash.
  - Correct radio/telephone procedures.
  - Correct use of challenge and password.
  - Light and noise discipline.
- Ensure that weapons and equipment are clean and serviceable.

- Establish and maintain field sanitation measures.

- Provide for periods of rest to the maximum extent possible, consistent with security measures and actions to prepare for the attack.

- Designate segregation area for equipment not required in the assault.

- Direct the drawing and distribution of ammunition, pyrotechnics, rations, water, and special equipment.

- Report at the designated time and place to receive the company commander's order.

- Conduct troop leading steps as described in appendix A.

- Receive attached units.

- Conduct a final communications check.

- Conduct specialized training and/or rehearsals.

DAYLIGHT ATTACK

On receipt of the company commander's order, the rifle platoon commander will —

- Take the platoon sergeant, one radio operator/messenger, and the forward observer (if available).

- Take maps, binoculars, notebooks, and pencils, and arrange a time and place for detailed coordination with adjacent and supporting unit leaders or their representatives.

- Begin planning:

- Using METT-T, make a preliminary estimate of the situation based on —
  - The intent of the company commander and the task he has assigned in the operation order.
  - A map and visual reconnaissance conducted during the company commander's orientation.
- Allocate time for personal reconnaissance and planning, subordinate leader reconnaissance and planning, and movement of the platoon forward to the assembly area when not concurrent with planning.
- Formulate tentative plan for attack.

■ Arrange for —
- Movement of the platoon forward from the assembly area, to include where, when, and how.
- A reconnaissance route and schedule to facilitate prearranged meetings with adjacent and supporting unit leaders for coordination.
- Participation of subordinate and attached unit leaders.

■ Make reconnaissance:
- Select a concealed vantage point from which to orient subordinate unit leaders, and a covered position nearby from which to issue the order.
- Notify subordinate unit leaders of the time and place where the platoon will receive the order.
- Determine enemy location, strength, and disposition.
- Determine key terrain features.

- Select intermediate objectives, where appropriate.
- Determine avenues of approach to the objectives.
- Select an assault position and other control measures when appropriate.
- Select a general position for base of fire and possible targets.
- Determine a route forward from the assembly area to the line of departure.
- Effect coordination in accordance with the prearranged schedule.

■ Complete the plan:
- Receive recommendation from supporting and/or attached unit leaders concerning the proposed employment of their units.
- Complete an estimate of the situation, to include actions required at the objective and exploitation and continuation of the attack.

■ Determine the scheme of maneuver:
- Determine the main effort and supporting efforts.
- Determine the form of maneuver based on available avenues of approach, enemy situation, and the desired effect on the enemy force.
- Plan for breaching, crossing, or bypassing known obstacles.
- Select the initial platoon formation based on the following:
  - Terrain.
  - Enemy situation.

- Security.
- Control.
- Flexibility.
- Speed.

• Employ tactical control measures, as appropriate, including —

- Intermediate objectives.
- Time of attack.
- Attack position.
- Line of departure (LD).
- Phase lines, checkpoints, or limit of advance.
- Boundaries.
- Base squad.
- Assault position.

• Provide for the additional security of the maneuver units by employing scouting elements forward and assigning overlapping sectors of observation.

• Integrate fires of supporting effort (base of fire) with assaulting units.

• Determine tasks for subordinate and attached units to include —

- Designation of a defensive position on the objective for each squad.
- Designation of general areas and specific missions for attached and/or direct support units.
- Security measures.

• Determine a fire support plan:

- Determine the extent to which planned fires support the platoon scheme of maneuver.
- Request additional fires, as necessary.
- Designate base of fire unit(s) to supplement other fires.
    - Establish positive fire control measures, to include time of signal for fires, rate of fire, safety limits, and time and/or signal for lifting or shifting fires.
    - Determine general positions and specific targets for base of fire unit(s).
    - Determine the method of displacement for the base of fire, to include time and/or signal for displacement forward, route of displacement, and displacement objective.
- Determine locations for corpsmen.
- Ensure that all pertinent extracts from the company commander's orders are considered in completing plans.
- Prescribe a location and special control functions for the platoon sergeant.
- Determine your own position from which the attack can best be controlled.

- Issue the order:
  - Orient subordinate unit leaders using a map and/or terrain model.
  - Ensure a thorough understanding of the orientation.
  - Utilize the standard order format (see the Operation Order, appendix A, page A-6).

- Issue the order using the terrain model to walk subordinates through the plan.
- Ensure a thorough understanding of the orders.

■ Supervise —

- Subordinate unit leader planning and the issuance of orders.
- Preparations for the attack.
- Rehearsals.

■ Conduct the attack:

- Ensure timely deployment of the platoon into the proper attack formation prior to crossing the line of departure.
- Ensure leading elements cross the line of departure at the time of attack.
- Maintain control and coordination utilizing the assistance of the platoon sergeant and squad leaders.
- Continue the estimate of the situation throughout the attack, and revise the plan as necessary through the use of fragmentary orders.
- Request supporting fires, as necessary.
- Notify the company commander of all bypassed enemy.
- Comply with control instructions regarding phase lines and checkpoints.
- Deploy assault elements upon reaching the assault position.
- Ensure commencement of the assault at the prescribed time or on a prearranged signal.

- Ensure the cessation or shift of supporting fire at the prescribed time or on a prearranged signal.

- Maintain assault formation and momentum of the assault through the assigned objective.

- Conduct pursuit by fire, to include employment of supporting fires.

- Report seizure of the objective to the company commander.

- Displace the remainder of the unit forward to predesignated locations on the prearranged signal.

- Reorganize promptly to reestablish subordinate chains of command and replace key billets made vacant by casualties.

- Establish local security, as required.

- Report the situation to the company commander, to include information concerning the enemy situation, friendly casualties, ammunition status, prisoners of war, captured documents, and significant material.

- Expedite casualty and ammunition status reports from subordinates.

- Redistribute ammunition.

- Evacuate casualties.

- Evacuate prisoners of war.

- In accordance with assigned mission, either continue the attack through issuance of a fragmentary order or supervise the continued organization of the ground for the defense.

NIGHT ATTACK

In the nonilluminated night attack, the following special considerations are integrated with the procedures prescribed for the daylight attack on page 1-21. The rifle platoon commander will —

- Prepare a plan:
  - Plan and conduct reconnaissance to —
    - Locate the platoon attack position.
    - Determine the point of departure on the line of departure (LD) if not assigned by the company commander.
    - Select the squad release point.
    - Locate assigned portion of the probable line of deployment (PLD).
    - Locate assigned portion of the company objective.
    - Select route from platoon release point through squad release point to PLD.
    - Locate prominent terrain features to guide movement and assist in identification of control points.
    - Determine azimuths, as appropriate.
    - Select limit of advance if not determined by the company commander.
  - Organize, coordinate, and dispatch security and reconnaissance patrols, as directed by the company commander, to include instructions on —
    - Reconnoitering and confirming the route from the platoon release point to the assigned portion of the PLD, and marking the route and control points for night identification, as necessary.

- Establishing security in the vicinity of the PLD to maintain continuous surveillance.
- Eliminating enemy in the vicinity of the assigned portion of the PLD at the prescribed time or on order.
- Returning at least one guide upon completion of reconnaissance by a prescribed time, with complete information including —
  - Marking and adjusting of the route and control points.
  - Enemy situation, to include assistance required to secure the assigned portion of the PLD.
  - Location of obstacles and the recommended measures to overcome them.
  - Location of remaining patrol members.
- Ensuring that all patrol members are familiar with landmarks and route to the PLD in dusk and darkness.
- Submitting patrol overlay by a prescribed time to permit coordination of routes, checkpoints, rally points, and the company fire support plan.
- Rejoining the platoon during execution of the attack.

• Report information from patrol findings and the platoon plan of attack to the company commander.

• If necessary, plan the use of a combat patrol in securing the assigned portion of the PLD just prior to the platoon's arrival. Coordinate the plan with the company commander.

• Coordinate with the appropriate platoon commanders concerning —
- Movement and routes if separate columns are used.
- Unit contact on the PLD and in consolidation.
- Guiding on the base platoon.

- Mutual recognition procedures.

• Plan for terrain orientation during daylight, dusk, and darkness by subordinate unit leaders, to include the use of selected vantage points and security precautions relative to movement and exposure.

• Select base squad(s) for movement forward, deployment on the PLD, and the assault. Include specific instructions for guiding on adjacent platoons during movement.

• Determine squad positions within the platoon column based on the sequence of release.

• Assign security missions to subordinate units in conjunction with their tactical missions.

  - In company column, assign one squad to provide at least one fire team for forward or flank security for column, as prescribed.
  - In platoon column, assign one squad to provide up to one fire team for forward security, and other squads to provide flank and rear security through designated sector of observation.
  - Assign all physical security responsibilities to the limit of observation.
  - Assign a patrol guide with forward security elements.

• Prescribe control measures as necessary and in consonance with those prescribed by the company commander. These include —

  - Control points.
  - Flare discipline.
  - Individual conduct.

- Movement forward from the PLD, on order.
- Commencement of assault fires.
- Mutual recognition procedures for patrol members and all leaders down to and including squad leaders.
- Primary and alternate signals to control movement and fire support.
- Actions on discovery, both prior to reaching the squad release point and after passing the squad release point.

• Plan for infiltration of and deployment on the enemy side of obstacles in the vicinity of the PLD.

• Plan for special measures to be taken for individual camouflage, silencing of equipment and clothing, and the segregation of equipment not required for the attack.

• Plan a rehearsal of the platoon for night attack.

■ Prepare for the attack:

• Brief the entire platoon on details of the operation.

• Conduct a rehearsal with particular attention to troop familiarity concerning —

- Flare discipline.
- Individual conduct, to include movement, maintaining distances and intervals, and light and noise discipline.
- Security measures.
- Radio discipline.
- Signals and visual identification code.
- Action on discovery prior to and after reaching control points, to include deployment, advance by fire, and maneuver to the PLD.
- Action after crossing the PLD.
- Action on the objective.

RIFLE PLATOON — Offensive Combat

- Supervise troop preparations to include —
    - Implementing individual camouflage.
    - Silencing equipment and clothing.
    - Removing or dulling shiny items.
    - Segregating equipment not required for the attack.
    - Issuing ammunition and pyrotechnics.
    - Conducting weapons checks.

- Conduct the attack:

    - Rejoin guide(s) and take appropriate action based on the latest patrol information.

    - Advance, guiding on the base platoon. The base platoon will maintain the direction and rate of advance.

    - Exercise strict noise, light, radio, and flare discipline throughout movement to the PLD.

    - Upon discovery by the enemy —
        - *Prior to reaching the platoon release point* take action as directed by the company commander.
        - *Between the platoon release point and squad release point* deploy squads as necessary and advance by fire and movement to PLD as necessary.
        - *After passing the squad release point* squad leaders take same action as in the paragraph above.

    - Eliminate enemy elements of the assigned portion of the PLD, if required.

    - Reform security elements of the patrol at the PLD.

- Ensure the deployment of squads on the PLD and report readiness to the company commander.

- On order —

  - Move silently forward from the PLD.
  - Assume assault formation.
  - Maintain intervals between individuals and units.
  - Upon discovery by the enemy, or on signal, commence fire and aggressive movement forward.
  - Assault through the objective to the predesignated limit of advance.
  - Conduct consolidation.

MECHANIZED INFANTRY ATTACK

Mechanized operations may be employed in all phases of offensive combat. These operations utilize basic forms of maneuver and formations. However, speed and mobility are greatly increased. The infantry platoon is employed as part of a mechanized task force, and the following special considerations are integrated with the procedures prescribed for the daylight attack on page 1-21.

In a mechanized infantry attack the platoon will be part of a mechanized infantry company team or tank company team. The rifle platoon will normally be transported in assault amphibious vehicles (AAVs). An AAV will contain 13 to 25 embarked personnel with tactical integrity maintained when possible. Generally, three AAVs support a rifle platoon. The senior unit commander embarked commands the vehicle in tactical situations.

The rifle platoon commander will —

- Confer with the supporting AAV unit leader to —
  - Exchange information on friendly and enemy situations.
  - Coordinate communications, to include netting infantry, tank, and AAV radios and exchanging call signs.
  - Plan reconnaissance.
- Conduct reconnaissance with AAV unit leaders:
  - Determine the extent and location of obstacles and enemy antitank defense.
  - Determine with the AAV unit leader the tentative tactical control measures including —
    - Attack position.
    - Line of departure.
    - Platoon axis of advance or zone of action, as appropriate.
    - Assault position.
    - Objective.
    - Limit of advance.
  - Determine the most feasible method of attack based on —
    - Mission.
    - Terrain and maneuver space.
    - Enemy.
    - Formation employed by the rifle company and platoon.
    - Movement techniques, mutual support, and security during movement and extended halts.
    - Communications during movement or when dismounted.
    - Reduction of obstacles and enemy antitank defenses.
    - Employment of combat support elements attached or in direct support.
    - Employment of nonorganic fire support.

- Coordinate the planning for seizure of the objective by receiving recommendations, as appropriate, on —
    - Assault positions.
    - Mission of AAVs after infantry dismounts. These missions include supporting attacks by fire, assisting in organization of the ground for the defense, or continuing the attack, as required.

INFANTRY/TANK ATTACKS

Infantry in the Lead

Dismounted infantry may lead tank units in the attack when dictated by METT-T. Restricted terrain reduces the observation of tank crews, the standoff range of the tank's main gun in close combat, and the speed with which the tank unit may move without becoming increasingly susceptible to ambush by enemy infantry antitank weapons. The rifle platoon may be employed to uncover and clear enemy infantry to allow the movement of the tank unit through this restricted terrain.

Tanks in the Lead

Infantry mounted in AAVs may follow tank units in the attack, or they may attack along a complementary axis when the terrain is relatively open to strike the objective from a different direction.

The following special considerations are integrated with the troop leading procedures for the daylight attack (page 1-21) and mechanized attacks (page 1-33). The rifle platoon commander will —

RIFLE PLATOON　　　　　　　**1-36**　　　　　　　**Offensive Combat**

- Confer with the tank unit commander to exchange information on the friendly and enemy situations and plan joint reconnaissance.
- Conduct joint reconnaissance with the tank unit leader:
  - Determine the extent and location of obstacles and enemy antitank defenses.
  - Identify tentative tactical control measures including —
    - Attack position.
    - Line of departure.
    - Assault position.
    - Terrain objective.
    - Limit of advance.
- Complete the plan to include —
  - Method of attack after dismount.
  - Initial attack formation.
  - Provision for positive control and communications.
    - Assign squads to AAVs and load them in the order of anticipated commitment.
    - Use visual signals and arrange with the AAV unit leader to use AAV radios while mounted.
    - Use radio, visual signals, and messenger when dismounted.
    - Use panels, smoke, and pyrotechnics for signalling and recognition.
  - Plan immediate actions upon dismounting during the advance.
  - Plan actions at the dismount area.
  - Provide for mutual support by fire.

- Issue the order to subordinate leaders and AAV/tank leaders.

ATTACK OF FORTIFIED AREAS

In the attack of fortified areas, the following special considerations are integrated with the procedures for the daylight attack on page 1-21. The rifle platoon commander will —

- Conduct a detailed reconnaissance to determine the location and extent of —
  - Individual emplacements to include —
    - Type or construction.
    - Number of embrasures.
    - Types of weapons and their fields of fire.
    - Entrances, exits, and air vents.
    - Location and extent of defending troops providing supporting small arms fire.
  - Supporting fortifications in assigned and adjacent zones.
  - Underground fortifications.
  - Natural and artificial obstacles.
  - Surfaces and gaps in the enemy defense.
  - Communications between emplacements.
  - Location of reserves
  - Positions for your own fire support units.
- Develop a detailed plan of attack which provides for —
  - Obstacle breaching.

- Emplacement seizure or destruction in the most effective sequence.
- Simultaneous seizure or destruction of mutually supporting emplacements, when feasible.
- Approach from the rear or blind side of emplacements.
- Seizure and defense of the assigned terrain objective.
- Clearing of the platoon zone of action.
- A reserve squad to —
  - Assume the mission of either attacking squad, as required.
  - Protect the flanks and rear of the platoon.
  - Prevent reoccupation of emplacements and destruction of bypassed enemy units, as required.
- Fires to provide —
  - Support of obstacle breaching operations.
  - Simultaneous engagement of all embrasures and supporting positions of the emplacements under attack.
  - Sequence of fires to ensure mutual support to the advance of attacking units.
- Task-organization of attacking squads, to include flame and demolition capability.

- Direct special training in the employment of flame weapons and demolitions.

- Plan and conduct a rehearsal with emphasis on timing, signals, and coordinated actions with adjacent and supporting units.

ATTACK OF URBAN TERRAIN

In the attack of built-up areas, the following special considerations are integrated with the procedures for the daylight attack on page 1-21. The rifle platoon commander will —

- Include in the estimate of the situation military aspects peculiar to the type of built-up area.
- Conduct a detailed reconnaissance in order to —
  - Determine buildings and terrain features within the platoon zone of action for assignment as squad objectives.
  - Locate key buildings and/or key terrain in the zone of action.
  - Select a reserve squad and fire support positions from which all-round security can be effected, including protection from above and below.
  - Locate killing zones.
- Formulate a plan of attack to include —
  - Considering flank and rear security.
  - Assigning a well-defined objective.
    - Number the buildings for ease of identification.
    - Designate large buildings, railroad crossings, or buildings at cross streets as single objectives.
    - Establish a sequence for seizure of buildings which affords maximum mutual support between attacking squads.
  - Assigning squad missions and frontages consistent with the type of construction encountered.

- Assigning directions of attack for squads which will minimize or avoid movement in streets, open areas, and enemy mutually supporting positions.
- Clearing the entire platoon zone of action, including bypassed buildings.
- Using the prescribed marking code for identification of cleared buildings.
- Constructing a fire support plan that provides —
  - Killing zones for machine guns.
  - Use of rocket launchers, tanks, and other direct fire weapons for breaching building entries and barricades.
  - Use of indirect fire weapons for defiladed areas, deeper targets away from the proximity of friendly and enemy troops, and for smoke and illumination.
  - Coordinating mutual fire support between attacking and adjacent units.
- Establishing alternate means of communication to compensate for the effect of buildings on line-of-sight radios.

■ Obtain the required equipment/munitions to include —

- Rope, ladders, and grappling hooks.
- An adequate supply of grenades, AT-4s, small arms ammunition, shoulder-launched multipurpose assault weapon (SMAW) ammunition, and satchel/demolition charges.

■ Conduct a detailed briefing of the platoon in conjunction with issuing the order to include —

- Layout of the built-up area in the platoon zone.

- Construction and interior layout of buildings whenever possible.
- Thorough understanding of the building marking code and signals.
- Known enemy boobytrap techniques.
- Known or suspected enemy strongpoints in the platoon zone.
- Building/room clearing techniques.

■ Segregate and stage equipment not required.

RIVER-CROSSING OPERATIONS

In river crossing operations, the following special considerations are integrated with the procedures prescribed for the daylight attack on page 1-21. The rifle platoon commander will —

■ Plan and conduct reconnaissance with the assault amphibious vehicle (AAV) section leader in order to —

- Determine the route forward from the assembly area to the platoon release point.
- Select AAV release points and the route forward from the platoon release point to the river-entry area.
- Confirm conditions of the river and its banks, as well as the location of obstacles, to include those underwater. Particular attention must be given to the direction and speed of the current.
- Select specific AAV launching points at the designated platoon entry site.

- Determine improvements necessary for the use of selected points.
- Select specific AAV landing points at the designated platoon landing site.

■ Coordinate planning with the AAV section leader to include —

- Marking of control points, as necessary.
- Entry of AAVs into the water in sequence from crossing points.
- Timing of entry into the water with adjacent units.
- Appropriate formation to compensate for drift.
- Use of vehicle mounted machine guns.
- Use of communication equipment.
- Loading of vehicles, to include rehearsals.
- Action in the event of vehicular casualty afloat.
- Action in the event of vehicle failure to negotiate the bank at the landing site.
- Actions on unloading.

■ Formulate a plan of attack to include —

- Order of the march from the assembly area which will facilitate continuous movement throughout the river crossing.
- Preservation of squad integrity and dispersion of crew-served weapons in boat team assignments.
- Launching and landing points for each AAV.
- Initial squad actions ashore.

- Measures for rapid reestablishment of control ashore.

- Instructions for the conduct of rehearsals, to include time, resupply, and equipment.

- Follow-up on secondary missions for AAVs. Some secondary missions that may be assigned are casualty evacuation, resupply, and reembarkation of troops for transportation to secondary objectives.

■ Ensure the AAV section leader and crew chiefs are present when issuing the attack order.

■ Conduct a full-scale rehearsal to simulate the crossing.

Defensive Combat

In addition to the general duties prescribed on page 1-1, the rifle platoon commander is responsible for the following actions during defensive combat.

FRONTLINE PLATOON

On receipt of the company commander's order, the rifle platoon commander will —

- Take a fire support representative (if assigned) and a messenger.
- Take maps, binoculars, notebooks, and pencils, and familiarize yourself with the company and battalion fire plans.
- Arrange for a time and place for detailed coordination with adjacent and supporting unit leaders or their representatives to include —
  - Weapons and/or personnel to be located or moved into the platoon position.
  - Location and extent of barrages and concentrations in the platoon area of responsibility.
- Begin planning:
  - Allocate time for —
    - Personal reconnaissance and planning.
    - Subordinate leader reconnaissance and planning.
    - Movement of the platoon forward from the assembly area.

- Organization of the platoon defense area, to include submission of a defensive fire plan sketch.
- Using METT-T, make a preliminary estimate of the situation based on —
  - The content of the company commander's order.
  - A map and visual reconnaissance conducted during the company commander's orientation.

■ Arrange for —
- Movement of the platoon forward from the assembly area, to include where, when, and how.
- A reconnaissance route and schedule to facilitate coordination with adjacent unit leaders and leaders of supporting units to be positioned within the assigned defensive area.
- Participation of subordinate and attached unit leaders in the reconnaissance.

■ Make reconnaissance:
- Determine limits of the defense area, to include frontage, depth, and coordinating points.
- Determine the security area forward of the forward edge of the battle area (FEBA), to include effective ranges of organic weapons and limitations imposed by terrain features.
- Select an appropriate vantage point from which to issue the order, and notify subordinate unit leaders of the time and place to receive order.
- Evaluate the terrain considering OCOKA.

- Based on terrain analysis and assigned missions, select a defensive position and sector of fire for each squad which provides for —
  - Mutual support with adjacent units.
  - Fields of fire and observation.
  - Cover and concealment.
  - Communications.
  - Protection for crew-served weapons in the platoon defense area.
  - All-round security.

- Determine a sector of fire for each squad to include —
  - Lateral limits to provide mutual support and overlapping of fires to cover gaps between units.
  - Forward limit defined by terrain feature designation, within effective small arms range.
  - Principal direction of fire (PDF) and general locations of specific automatic rifles and grenade launchers to —
    - Cover gaps in the final protective line (FPL) and dead space in squad frontage.
    - Cover dangerous terrain features.
    - Protect crew-served weapons or cover obstacles.
    - Augment flanking fire across the front.
    - Supplement the fires of machine guns.
  - Integration with fires of crew-served weapons and other supporting weapons.

- Determine the general location of supplementary positions which —
  - Protect the flank or rear of the platoon position.

- Are within the limit of the platoon defense area.
- Protect supplementary positions of crew-served weapons.
- Afford covered/concealed approaches from the primary position.

• Determine requirements for additional fire support.

• Consider recommendations for adjustments of targets, final protective fires (FPFs), or FPLs necessary to provide optimum fire effect.

• Determine improvements to, or construction of, obstacles in coordination with the fire plan and the barrier plan of higher headquarters.

• Determine locations for prescribed local security:

- Sentinel Posts: during daylight hours; along most likely avenues of approach; positioned to provide maximum observation beyond intermittent terrain forward of the principal defensive positions; within effective range of supporting weapons to provide for the cover of the post during withdrawal.
- Listening Posts: during hours of reduced visibility; within direct fire range of the principal defensive postions; along likely avenues of approach.
- Patrols: conducted across front and open flanks in areas difficult to observe (may be farther when directed by higher echelon).

• Select a platoon observation post (OP) site that provides —

- Observation of the entire platoon front or the most dangerous avenue of approach.

- Space for dispersion of forward observers (FOs) in the platoon area.
- Concealment for supply activities.
- Covered/concealed approach from the rear.

• Coordinate, as prearranged with the adjacent and supporting unit leaders, on —
  - Fires to cover approaches or gaps.
  - Physically tie-in wherever possible.
  - Protection of crew-served weapons which may displace into positions located in the area of another unit.
  - Use and improvement of obstacles.
  - Adjustment of coordinating point(s), where necessary.

• Request additional fire, or adjustment of planned fires and coordinating point(s), from the company commander, as determined in reconnaissance and coordination.

- Complete the plan:
  • Assign a defensive mission to each squad to include —
    - Designating the squad defense position.
      · For close terrain, physically tie-in.
      · Lateral boundaries by terrain feature designation or relation to adjacent unit(s).
      · For open terrain, cover gaps by fire and observation.
      · Prescribe one- or two-man fighting holes, as appropriate.

- Designating the sector of fire, to include lateral boundaries by terrain designation, forward limit by terrain designation, principal direction of fire, and position of specific automatic rifles and grenade launchers.
- Assigning responsibility for establishing local security, to include the location of a sentinel and/or listening post and security patrols, when directed.
- Assigning responsibility to protect crew-served weapons, including the location of primary, alternate, and/or supplementary gun positions.
- Assigning responsibility for establishing obstacles.
  - Select a detail from the least engaged unit in terms of enemy threat.
  - Determine what, when, where, and how (type of obstacles, priority, location, and resources).

- Plan coordinating instructions to include —
  - Priority of work.
    - Post security.
    - Positioning of squad automatic weapons.
    - Clearance of fields of fire.
    - Construction of positions and emplacements.
    - Preparation of supplementary positions.
    - Construction of obstacles.
    - Improvements of camouflage.
    - Rehearsals.
  - Assignment of the platoon rear boundary by terrain designation.

- Plans for fire control, including final protective fire signal and alert conditions procedures for ground, air, and enemy nuclear, biological, and chemical (NBC) attacks.
- Procedure for the recall of local security.
- Night security measures, including movement, light and noise discipline, and challenge and password.
- Submission of squad fire plan sketches.

• Incorporate logistic considerations including —

- Tools and fortification materials available (what, when, where, allocation, and purpose).
- Ammunition, water, food, and radio batteries.
- Assignment of corpsmen and the location of the battalion aid station.

• Incorporate signals and communication means providing for —

- Fire control of close and final protective fires.
- Control of local security.
- Contact with higher, adjacent, supporting, and subordinate leaders.
- Warning of ground, armor, air, and enemy NBC attack.
- Location of the platoon command post (CP)/OP.
- Location of the company CP.

■ Issue the order:

• Orient subordinates thoroughly to include —

- Platoon defense and security area.
- Likely avenues of approach.
- Targets and FPFs.
- Obstacles.

- Terrain/vegetation
- Weather
- Known or suspected enemy positions
- Friendly positions

• Issue the order from a vantage point.

• Walk the ground with subordinates, as necessary, to point out —

- Specific location and limit of each squad position.
- Sector of fire for each squad.
- Location of obstacles to be constructed.
- Location of the PDF or FPL of crew-served weapons in the platoon defense area.

■ Supervise —

• Organization of the ground to include—

- Establishment of local security, as directed.
- Location and construction of fire team positions by the squad leaders.
- Protection of exposed flanks.
- Preparation of supplementary positions.

• Organization of fires to include—

- Positioning and assignment of the PDF for squad automatic weapons and grenade launchers (M203).
- Integration of organic fires with supporting fires and fires of adjacent units.
- Assignment of fire team sectors of fire.

• Construction of obstacles, as directed.

- Continuous camouflage measures.
- Establishment of communications.
- Distribution of supplies.
- Rehearsals
■ Submit a platoon fire plan sketch to include—
  - Primary and supplementary positions of each squad.
  - Sector of fire for each squad.
  - Location and PDF for all squad automatic weapons and grenade launchers.
  - Location and PDF or FPL of crew-served weapons in the platoon defense area.
  - Location of local security.
  - Targets and FPFs.
  - Location of the platoon CP/OP.
■ Conduct the defense:
  - Notify the company commander of enemy activity.
  - Recall local security on the approval of the company commander.
  - Fire close defensive fires, as planned.
  - Maintain fire discipline and control.
  - Request final protective fires when appropriate and/or fire final protective fires, as directed.

- Defend the platoon defense area by fire, close combat, and shifting to supplementary positions, as necessary.

- Inform the company commander of the situation at all times, including penetrations, occupation of supplementary positions, and crew-served weapons out of action.

- When the enemy is repelled —
  - Cease final protective fires, as directed.
  - Maintain pursuit by fire until targets cease to exist.
  - Reestablish local security, as directed.
  - Adjust weapons and troops, as necessary.
  - Redistribute ammunition.
  - Evacuate casualties.
  - Submit a situation report, to include enemy situation, casualties, ammunition status, prisoners of war, documents, and significant material.
  - Evacuate prisoners of war.

RESERVE PLATOON, FRONTLINE COMPANY

In the employment of the reserve platoon, the following special considerations are integrated with the procedures prescribed for the frontline platoon on page 1-44. The rifle platoon commander will —

- Support frontline platoons by fire:
  - Prepare the designated primary position.
  - Plan for overhead fires.
  - Plan fires to cover gaps, flanks, and rear of frontline platoons.
  - Coordinate the fire plan with frontline units.

- Limit penetrations:
  - Prepare the designated primary position.
  - Prepare supplementary positions, as directed.
  - Plan fires into probable areas(s) of penetration, as directed.
  - Coordinate the fire plan with affected units.
- Protect the company's flanks and rear:
  - Prepare the designated primary position.
  - Prepare supplementary positions covering avenues of approach.
  - Plan fires into probable avenues of approach.
  - Coordinate the fire plan with frontline and supporting units.
- Assign security and surveillance:
  - Provide personnel for patrols, as directed.
  - Provide personnel for sentinels and/or listening posts, as directed.
  - Ensure frequent reliefs of security and surveillance personnel.
  - Coordinate security and surveillance measures with the frontline unit.
- Counterattack:
  - Conduct reconnaissance of areas of probable penetration, to include locating the assigned line(s) of departure and knowing the disposition of frontline platoons.
  - Coordinate fire plans with affected units.

- Plan fires in support of the counterattack.
- Brief subordinate leaders.
- Conduct rehearsals with emphasis on individual aggressiveness and violence of action.
- Counterattack on order.

REVERSE SLOPE DEFENSE

In the organization for reverse slope defense, the following special considerations are integrated with the procedures prescribed for frontline platoon (page 1-44) and reserve platoon (page 1-53).

Frontline Platoon

The rifle platoon commander will —

- Establish observation and security groups forward of the topographical crest, as directed.

- Position squads to deliver maximum fire on the crest and the ground between the crest and the forward edge of the battle area (FEBA).

- Prepare dummy positions on the forward military crest, as directed.

Reserve Platoon

The rifle platoon commander will —

- Prepare the primary position on the military crest of the next high ground within supporting range behind the forward edge of the battle area (FEBA), as directed.

- Provide observation and security elements to operate in the company's security area.

- Plan fires to support frontline platoons, including engagement of enemy crossing the topographical crest and continuation of fires on the reverse slope until masked.

- Prepare counterattack plans to regain control of the topographical crest.

PLATOON AS A SECURITY FORCE

In the organization of a security force, the platoon may be tasked to perform the duties of a combat outpost. The following special considerations are integrated with procedures prescribed for the frontline platoon on page 1-44. The rifle platoon commander will —

- Coordinate with —
  - Adjacent unit leaders concerning security positions, patrol routes, and mutual support.
  - Supporting unit leaders concerning support of the position by fire and support of the withdrawal.
  - Covering force commander or representative, as directed.

- Conduct reconnaissance:
  - Select positions that provide long-range observation, long-range fires across the entire front, and visual contact between subordinate units.
  - Select patrol routes that provide for contact between positions when observation is limited, early warning of enemy approach, and contact with higher security forces.
- Prepare a fire plan:
  - Plan fires to include —
    - Long-range fires.
    - Fires between positions.
    - Maximum coverage by machine guns and squad automatic weapons.
    - Fires within positions.
  - Plan fires that provide for —
    - Delay of enemy advance.
    - Coverage of the covering force during its withdrawal.
    - Support of the security force withdrawal.
    - Mutual support between units.
    - Support of subsequent delaying actions.
- Conduct the plan:
  - Patrol between positions.
  - Cover the withdrawal of the covering force.
  - Withdraw patrols and local security as the enemy approaches.
  - Engage the enemy at maximum ranges, maintain pressure, and avoid close combat.

- Utilize supporting fires, as planned.
- Withdraw on order.

DEFENSE OF URBAN TERRAIN

In the defense of urban terrain, the following special considerations are integrated with the procedures prescribed for the frontline platoon on page 1-44. The rifle platoon commander will —

- Conduct reconnaissance:
  - Select key buildings in the assigned defense area.
  - Select local security positions which provide for securing ground level approaches, approaches from adjacent buildings above ground, and approaches from sewers, cellars, and other subsurface installations.
- Prepare a plan:
  - Assign each squad a building, or portion thereof, to defend.
    - Assign final protective lines (FPLs), when authorized, and principal direction of fires (PDFs) down streets and alleys.
    - Provide close-in protection for any crew-served weapons located in the platoon defense area, to include ground-level, overhead, and subsurface defense.
  - Assign position(s) and missions to any attached crew-served weapons.
  - Employ street barricades, mines, and other obstacles.
  - Barricade, boobytrap, and plan fires on buildings within the platoon defense area which are not occupied.

- Prepare occupied buildings for the defense by —
  - Barricading windows, doors, and other openings.
  - Removing drain pipes, vines, and projections which could assist the enemy in gaining outside access to the upper floors or roofs.
  - Sandbagging individual positions in upper floors for protection from fires from below.
  - Constructing individual barricades in rooms for protection.
- Report the location of all boobytraps to the company commander.

Relief Operations

In addition to the general duties prescribed on page 1-1, the rifle platoon commander is responsible for the following actions during relief operations.

RELIEF IN PLACE

Mutual Considerations of Incoming and Outgoing Rifle Platoon Commanders

- Exchange information concerning the enemy situation and area of operations.
- Effect close coordination and detailed planning relative to —
  - Time schedule.
  - Order and method of the relief of subordinate units.
  - Reconnaissance.
  - Exchange of weapons, equipment, and supplies.
  - Plan of action if attacked prior to completion of the relief.
  - Routes of ingress and egress, and the priority of their use.
  - Available communications.
- Exchange liaison NCOs to keep the unit leader abreast of the situation.
- Establish security measures, as necessary, to give the impression of normal activity.
- Plan for attachments during relief.
- Conduct a detailed briefing of subordinate leaders.
- Minimize movement on the forward edge of the battle area (FEBA).

Responsibilities of the Incoming Rifle Platoon Commander

- Establish command post (CP)/observation post (OP) in the CP/OP of the outgoing unit.

- Receive a briefing on the enemy situation and area of operations from the outgoing commander.

- Conduct daylight reconnaissance with emphasis on —
  - Defensive dispositions and the plans of the outgoing unit.
  - Terrain.
  - Exact locations of minefields, tactical wire, and associated lanes or gaps.
  - Location of the platoon release point.
  - Selection of squad release points and routes from the release points to positions.

- Leave liaison personnel at squad positions.

- Arrange for the exchange of equipment, supplies, and weapons on their tripods and base plates, if directed.

- Appoint a platoon liaison NCO.

- Arrange for daylight reconnaissance by subordinate and attached unit leaders.

- Receive guides from the outgoing unit.

- Establish a method and sequence of relief by squad.

- Relieve crew-served weapons crews after the relief of rifle units.

- Relieve the local security unit last.

- Notify the company commander when the relief is completed.
- Submit a fire plan sketch or overlay to the company commander.

Responsibilities of the Outgoing Rifle Platoon Commander

- Brief the incoming commander on the enemy situation and area of operations.
- Conduct your own reconnaissance with emphasis on the withdrawal routes, assembly areas, and new positions.
- Arrange for the exchange of equipment, supplies, and weapons on their tripods and base plates, if directed.
- Appoint a platoon liaison NCO.
- Appoint guides to lead the incoming unit into positions.
- Appoint guides to lead your own unit to the rear.
- Arrange for liaison personnel to remain in positions with the incoming unit throughout the relief (usually one per squad).
- Relieve the squad leader of responsibility for the position when the incoming squad is in place.
- Relieve local security units last.
- Relinquish responsibility for the area when agreed upon by both commanders and when verified by receiving the concurrence of their next higher commander.
- Move the platoon from its assembly area to the company assembly area.

PASSAGE OF LINES

In the passage of lines, the following special considerations are integrated with the procedures prescribed for the daylight attack (page 1-21) or the night attack (page 1-28), as appropriate.

Mutual Considerations of the Attacking Rifle Platoon Commander and the Platoon Commander of the Unit in Contact

- Exchange information on the enemy situation and the area of operations.

- Determine areas of passage.

- Coordinate passage through, or withdrawal of, local security, as appropriate.

- Coordinate administrative and logistic support for the attack, as directed.

- Coordinate transfer of responsibility for the zone (normally time of attack).

Responsibilities of the Attacking Rifle Platoon Commander

- Establish a command post (CP)/observation post (OP) near the CP/OP of the unit in contact.

- Receive a briefing concerning the enemy situation and area of operations from the platoon commander of the unit in contact.

- Conduct daylight reconnaissance with emphasis on —
  - Platoon and squad assembly areas.
  - Route(s) forward to the line of departure.

- Area(s) of passage.
- Gaps or lanes in minefields and wire obstacles.
- Location of the security positions of the unit in contact.

■ Receive guides from the unit in contact.

■ Arrange for daylight reconnaissance by subordinate and attached unit leaders.

■ Incorporate fire support available from the unit in contact into the plan of attack

Responsibilities of the Rifle Platoon Commander of the Unit in Contact

■ Brief the attacking commander on the enemy situation and area of operations.

■ Assist the attacking commander on his reconnaissance.

■ Provide guides to the attacking unit.

■ Provide administrative and logistic support, as directed.

■ Provide fires in direct support of the attacking unit in consonance with the prearranged plan.

Retrograde Operations

In addition to the general duties prescribed on page 1-1, the rifle platoon commander is responsible for the following actions during retrograde operations.

NIGHT WITHDRAWAL

The rifle platoon commander will —

- Issue the warning order to provide for maximum use of daylight for preparation, reconnaissance, subordinate planning, and reasons for movement.

- Prepare a plan to include —

  - Designating a squad as the detachment left in contact.

  - Conducting personal reconnaissance, if the situation permits, with emphasis on —
    - Location of the platoon assembly area.
    - Route to the company assembly area.
    - Selection of squad assembly areas.
    - Selection of squad routes from the squad assembly areas to the platoon assembly area.

  - Appointing guides for the withdrawal routes and assembly areas, as necessary.

  - Attaching and employing crew-served weapon units located in the platoon area for withdrawal.

  - Providing security patrols, as directed.

- Providing for flexibility and decentralized control by conducting a thorough briefing of subordinate and attached unit leaders, making preparations to use daylight techniques, and preparing alternate plans as time permits.

- Coordinating plans when withdrawing through a friendly unit, to include mutual recognition signals, routes of withdrawal, areas of passage, responsibility for the zone of action.

■ Conduct the plan:

- Relinquish control of the detachment left in contact to the company detachment commander on order.

- Position guides, as required.

- Commence withdrawal to the assembly areas at a designated time or on order.

- Destroy supplies and equipment which cannot be evacuated.

- Ensure rapid, quiet movement during withdrawal.

- When withdrawing through a friendly unit, pass through rapidly and notify the friendly unit commander when the last element has effected passage.

DAYLIGHT WITHDRAWAL

Frontline Platoon

The rifle platoon commander will —

■ Issue a warning order to provide for subordinate planning and reasons for movement.

- Prepare a plan to include —
  - Conducting personal reconnaissance if the situation permits, with emphasis on the zone of action, location of the platoon assembly area, and route(s) to the company assembly area.
  - Selecting withdrawal routes within the designated zone, rally points for the squads, and successive covering positions, as directed.
  - Appointing a subordinate as the platoon representative in the company reconnaissance party, as directed.
  - Establishing a sequence of withdrawal.
  - Providing for flexibility and decentralized control by conducting a thorough briefing of subordinate and attached unit leaders and preparing alternate plans as time permits.
  - Coordinating plans when withdrawing through a friendly unit, to include mutual recognition signals, routes of withdrawal, areas of passage, responsibility for the zone of action, and priority on the use of routes in the rear.
- Conduct the operation:
  - Commence the withdrawal at the designated time or on order while being covered by the covering force.
  - Destroy supplies and equipment which cannot be evacuated.
  - Select crew-served weapons to remain forward until the last units withdraw.
  - When withdrawing through a friendly unit, pass through rapidly and notify friendly unit commander when the last element has executed passage.

Reserve Platoon

In the daylight withdrawal of the reserve platoon, the following special considerations are integrated with the procedures prescribed for the daylight withdrawal of the frontline platoon on page 1-66. The rifle platoon commander will —

- Coordinate with the frontline platoon commander concerning administrative and logistic support requirements of the frontline platoons, as directed, and fire support requirements.

- Formulate a detailed plan of covering fires in support of the withdrawal in consonance with prior coordinated agreements.

DELAYING ACTION

In the delaying action, the following special considerations are integrated with the procedures prescribed for the defense (page 1-44) and withdrawal (page 1-65). The rifle platoon leader will —

- Prepare a plan to include —
  - Conducting a personal reconnaissance with emphasis on —
    - Location and extent of initial delaying position.
    - Location and extent of subsequent delaying positions(s).
    - Availability of observation and fields of fire from topographical crest.
    - Location of rally points and withdrawal routes between positions.
  - Organizing the ground on or near the topographical crest.

- Engaging the enemy by fire at maximum range.
- Conduct the plan:
  - Engage the enemy by fire at maximum range.
  - Avoid close combat.
  - Execute the planned withdrawal.
  - Keep selected crew-served weapons forward until the last units withdraw.

Mine Warfare

In addition to the general duties prescribed on page 1-1, the rifle platoon commander is responsible for the following actions during mine warfare.

CONVENTIONAL MINEFIELD INSTALLATION

Table 1-1 describes some of the different types and characteristics of minefields.

TYPE	DESCRIPTION	TACTICAL USE	REPORTS REQUIRED
Hasty Protective	Above ground random pattern. No antihandle devices.	Aids in unit local close-in protection of defensive perimeter.	Intention Initiation Completion Change/Removal
Deliberate Protective	Standard Pattern/ Fenced and Marked	Same as above.	Same as above.
Nuisance	Standard or reform pattern/scat	As part of obstacle plan.	Same as above.
Point	Random pattern/ Surface or buried	Enhance obstacles. Hinder use of key areas.	Same as above.
Interdict	Placed on or behind enemy locale.	Separate, destroy, and disrupt the enemy.	Same as above.
Phony	Same as live minefield being simulated.	Simulate other minefields.	Same as that simulated.

Table 1-1. Minefield Types and Characteristics

Minefields require emplacement authority as shown in table 1-2.

Level	Conventional Minefields		Scatterable Mines/ Duration		Other Obstacles	
	Tact	Protect	Long	Short	Tact	Protect
MEF	X	X	X	X	X	X
DIVISION	X	X	X	X	X	X
REGIMENT	X	X	X	X	X	X
BATTALION		X			X	X
COMPANY		X				X

Table 1-2. Obstacle Emplacement Authority

There are four types of conventional minefield reports that must be completed when emplacing a hasty protective minefield. All minefields are reported by the fastest means available and are classified SECRET when completed.

EXPLANATION	LETTER DESIGNATOR	EXAMPLE
Tactical objectives (temporary security roadblock or other)	Alpha	Bridge work site security.
Type of minefield	Bravo	Hasty protective.
Estimated number and types of mines and whether surface laid mines or mines with antihandling devices	Charlie	10 each M18A1 No AHD
Location of minefield by coordinates	Delta	UTO96764
Location and width of minefield lanes and gaps	Echo	Rt. 67 North-south approach to bridge
Estimated starting and completion date-time group	Foxtrot	Start 190700 May 94 Completion 191000 May 94

Table 1-3. Report of Intention To Lay with Example

EXPLANATION	LETTER DESIGNATOR	EXAMPLE
Location of minefield by coordinates	Delta	UTO96764
Estimated starting and completion date-time group	Foxtrot	Start 190700 May 94 Completion 191000 May 94

Table 1-4. Report of Initiation with Example

EXPLANATION	LETTER DESIGNATOR	EXAMPLE
Location of minefield by coordinates, 25% completed	Delta	UT096764, 25% completed.

Table 1-5. Report of Progress with Example

EXPLANATION	LETTER DESIGNATOR	EXAMPLE
Changes in information submitted in intention to lay report	Alfa	None
Total number and type of AT and AP mines laid	Bravo	M15 – 299 M26 – 865 M14 – 601
Date and time of completion	Charlie	231800 Mar 87
Method of laying mines (buried by hand or machine)	Delta	Buried by hand
Details of lanes and gaps including marking	Echo	WD1 wire on $\mathcal{C}$ AZ.270° Ent and Ex marked with 2U pickets
Details of perimeter marking	Foxtrot	Standard fence
Overlay showing perimeter, lanes, and gaps	Golf	NA
Laying unit and signature of individual authorizing laying of the field	Hotel	2d Pit. Co A. 546th Engr Bn (C)

Table 1-6. Report of Completion of Minefield with Example

If the minefield changes, or if an area is taken over by another unit, the following reports must be made:

- A *transfer report* is used when minefield responsibility is transferred between commanders. This report certifies the receiving commander was shown or informed of all mines within the zone of action or sector and takes full responsibility for those mines. It is sent to the higher commander who has the authority of both the relieved and relieving commanders.

- A *change report* is submitted when any alterations are made to a minefield for which a completion report and record have been submitted.

Hasty protective minefields are normally the only type of minefields which a platoon may be tasked to emplace without engineer assistance. To install a hasty protective minefield, the rifle platoon commander will —

- Conduct a thorough leader's reconnaissance of the proposed minefield area.

- Utilize DA form 1355-1-R (see tables 1-7 and 1-8).

- Emplace and mark the mines without arming.

- Identify an easily identifiable reference point between the minefield and the unit position. The row of mines closest to the enemy is row A; succeeding rows are designated B, C, D, and so on. The ends of the rows are indicated by markers labeled with the row's letter and the numbers 1 (for one end of the row) and 2 (for the other end of the row). The marker should be an easily identifiable object, such as a wooden stake or steel picket.

- Measure the distance and azimuth between each mine until all mines, in each row, have been recorded. Assign each mine a number as it is recorded. The distance and azimuth between the reference point and a landmark are recorded.

- Arm mines after the recording is completed. Mines closest to the enemy are armed first. Engineer tape or other markings should be removed as mines are armed.

- Collect safety pins and clips from the laying party to verify the arming of mines. Secure pins and clips for future use.

MINEFIELD BREACHING

The rifle platoon commander will —

- Organize the platoon into support, breach, and assault parties:
  - The support party provides security for the breach party.
  - The assault party assaults the enemy position once the breach has been made.
- Designate a start point and direction to the breach party.
- Indicate a method and supervise the cleared lane marking.
- Ensure breached lanes are marked.
- Report completion of the breaching mission to the company commander.
- Leave a guide to hand over control of the breached lane(s) to follow-on forces.

Mob and Riot Control

In addition to the general duties prescribed on page 1-1, the rifle platoon commander is responsible for the following actions during mob and riot control. The rifle platoon commander will —

- Prepare a plan:
  - Review the company alert plan(s) and unit SOP(s).

- Plan the best use of available training time in consonance with the company training schedule.

■ Conduct training in —

- Proper riot control formations to ensure that movements are executed with precision, the platoon presents a military appearance, and all personnel thoroughly understand the individual movements in riot control formations.
- Crowd and mob behavior.
- Preparation and use of riot control agents.
- Use of any available riot control equipment.

■ Wear field protective masks during riot control exercises.

■ Conduct a thorough briefing of squad leaders on missions stated in the company alert plan(s).

■ Conduct detailed rehearsals of contingency plans and SOPs.

- Select and train marksmen.
- Conduct training with bayonet and close combat fighting techniques.
- Conduct training in the establishment and defense of roadblocks and street barricades.

■ Conduct the operations:

- Issue the warning order.
- Study available intelligence for current information.
- Form the unit, as directed.
- On order, perform one or more of the following missions:

- Construct and defend a roadblock or street barricade.
- Conduct a show of force.
    - Form the platoon in the assembly area out of sight of the rioters.
    - Fix bayonets and place loaded magazines in the weapon, bolt home, chamber empty, and weapon on safe.
    - March the platoon in formation to a position in plain view of the mob but at a safe distance.
    - Halt the platoon in formation with weapons at high port.
    - The senior commander will issue the proclamation to disperse, the time allowed in which to disperse, and which route to follow in leaving the area.
    - If the rioters disperse, follow them to the designated phase line.
- Employ riot control formations to disperse the mob, as directed.
- Employ riot control agents, as directed.
- On the order of the senior commander, direct rounds to be chambered with the weapon on safe.
- On the order of the senior commander, direct preselected marksmen to fire at specific targets authorized under the criteria for use of deadly force.

Noncombatant Evacuation Operations

In addition to the general duties prescribed on page 1-1, the rifle platoon commander is responsible for the following actions during noncombatant evacuation operations.

TRAINING

The rifle platoon commander will —

- Conduct training with emphasis on —

  - Recognizing the differences between a permissive and non-permissive environment.

  - Understanding the purpose of established rules of engagement.

  - Familiarizing small units with noncombatant evacuation operation (NEO) force organization, and the functions of major components to include —

    - Security element.
    - Command element.
    - Evacuation control center element.
    - Dismount station.
    - Search station.
    - Screening station.
    - Processing stations.
    - Embark station.
    - Holding areas.
    - Medical stations.

- Preparing small units for the unique/difficult situations that individual Marines encounter while handling diplomats, U.S. citizens, foreign nationals, and other civilians during NEO operations.
- Preparing squads for dealing with the media, including orienting Marines on what to expect when being interviewed.

PLANNING AND CONDUCT OF THE MISSION

The rifle platoon commander will —

- Plan for operations in a nonpermissive environment.
- Determine and disseminate rules of engagement (ROE). Test familiarity with ROE through situational practical application drills.
- Establish a clear/simple plan for communications, command, and control.
- Establish clear/simple immediate action procedures.
- Plan for a withdrawal under pressure.
- Establish clear/concise procedures for reception of evacuees aboard amphibious shipping, if applicable.

Humanitarian Assistance/Disaster Relief

In addition to the general duties prescribed on page 1-1, the rifle platoon commander is responsible for the following actions during humanitarian assistance and disaster relief.

TRAINING

The rifle platoon commander will —

- Prepare small units for extensive interaction with the local populace, to include information on —
  - Local political situation.
  - Local customs, traditions, and culture.
  - Local religious practices/beliefs and respective sensitivity to Western beliefs/behavior.
  - Local economic situation/standard of living.
  - Local perceptions of the Western world and the expected reaction to the presence of U.S. forces.
  - Effects on the local populace of recent civil unrest/military operations.
- Familiarize squads with the potential for a nonpermissive environment and the resulting ramifications for maintaining the overall security of the force.

PLANNING AND CONDUCT OF THE MISSION

The rifle platoon commander will —

- Establish and disseminate clear/concise rules of engagement (ROE).
- Task-organize the platoon and attachments in accordance with METT-T.
- Rehearse squads for the tasks/missions that are inherently foreign to infantry units.
- Establish a clear and simple plan for command, control, and communications.
- Familiarize the platoon with daily health and hygiene precautions to be taken in the host country.

CHAPTER 2

RIFLE SQUAD

The **mission** of the **rifle squad** is to locate, close with, and destroy the enemy by fire and maneuver, or repel the enemy's assault by fire and close combat.

This chapter discusses the duties of the **rifle squad leader**

General Duties

In addition to the procedures prescribed for all troop leaders in appendix A, the rifle squad leader will —

- Conduct tactical training of the rifle squad in accordance with platoon training directives.

- Control the tactical employment of the rifle squad in combat and training operations through the use of appropriate troop leading procedures.

- Revise estimates of the situation continually during the conduct of operations in order to more effectively accomplish assigned tactical missions.

- Coordinate the employment of the rifle squad, as authorized, with units supporting the squad mission.

- Supervise and control the safeguarding and economical use of supplies and equipment.

- Supervise first echelon maintenance of weapons and equipment through frequent inspection.

- Provide information, as directed, for inclusion in platoon records and reports.

Amphibious Operations

In addition to the duties prescribed on page 2-1, the rifle squad leader is responsible for performing the following actions during amphibious operations.

PRE-EMBARKATION DUTIES

The rifle squad leader will —

- Conduct training:
  - Ensure that the squad attends all instruction.
  - Assist the platoon commander in conducting and supervising individual and unit training, as directed.
  - Ensure that the fire team leaders are proficient in fire team and squad tactics.
  - Conduct critiques of squad training and initiate corrective action, as required.
  - Make recommendations to the platoon commander on training deficiencies within the squad.

- Conduct inspections of weapons, clothing, and equipment to ensure preparedness for the operation and embarkation.

■ Supervise the marking/tagging of weapons, equipment, and baggage for embarkation, as directed.

■ Assemble the squad in proper uniform at the designated time for embarkation.

DUTIES ABOARD SHIP

The rifle squad leader will —

■ Assign fire team berthing areas and supervise stowage of gear.

■ Ensure the squad attends all briefings and periods of instruction.

■ Ensure the squad area is in a good state of police through the assignment of police details, close supervision, and frequent inspection.

■ Hold physical musters, as directed.

■ Enforce applicable ship's regulations.

■ Assist in conducting and supervising training to include —

- Physical conditioning exercises.
- Military subjects, stressing those which are important to the operation.
- Maintenance of weapons and equipment.

■ Direct and supervise the care and cleaning of weapons.

■ Supervise the security of individual weapons.

- Report all discrepancies in ship's facilities.
- Ensure correct conduct and appearance of the squad.
- Conduct operational planning:
  - Brief the squad on platoon and company missions and intents, scheduled rehearsals, debarkation procedures, and ship-to-shore movement.
  - Make a detailed study of maps, aerial photographs, mockups, and sketches.
  - Make a preliminary estimate of the situation.
  - Formulate a tentative plan of attack.
  - Submit the tentative plan of attack to the platoon commander.
  - Complete the tentative plan.
- Issue the order and ensure thorough understanding by utilizing mockups, sketches, maps, aerial photographs, and question and answer techniques.

DUTIES DURING SHIP-TO-SHORE MOVEMENT

The rifle squad leader will —

- Assemble the squad in the boat team assembly area.
- Prior to debarkation, inspect the squad for proper rigging of weapons and equipment.
- Carry out the duties of a boat team commander as described in appendix B, when so assigned.

- Assist the boat team commander in debarkation.

- Supervise the positioning of the squad in the landing craft, amphibious vehicle, or rigid raiding craft (RRC)/combat rubber raiding craft (CRRC).

- Review the details of such items as landing beach and surrounding terrain with fire team leaders.

- For RRC/CRRC, organize the squad into a boat team, as required. Each boat team member is trained to execute a specific task based on his position in the craft. (See table 2-1.)

POSITION	TITLE	TASKS
1	Stroke Man	Sets the paddle rate and maintains rhythm, as directed by coxswain. Assists coxswain in keeping the boat perpendicular to the breakers when beaching or launching. Helps avoid obstacles in the water and advises when to cut the engine. The stroke man is selected for strength and ability to maintain a steady rhythm.
2	Bowman	Handles bow line and assists the coxswain in keeping perpendicular to the breaker line. Helps avoid obstacles. Handles tow line and quick release.
3 and 4		Lashes and unloads equipment. Serve as scout swimmers during tactical boat landings if scout swimmers are not carried as passengers.
5 and 6		Assists in lashing and unloading equipment in the aft section of the boat. They assist coxswain in maneuvering in swift currents, and rig and handle the sea anchor whenever used.
7 and 8	Assistant and Coxswain	Responsible for the performance of the crew and handling of the boat. The coxswain distributes equipment and crew members in the boat, issues all commands to the crew members, and maintains course and speed.

Figure 2-1. Boat Team Positions and Tasks.

- For RRC/CRRC, review the following tactical considerations:
  - Location, type, and range of enemy sensors, alarms, or radar.
  - Patrols near the beach landing site.
  - Schedules and routes of patrol craft.
  - Schedules and capabilities of air patrols.
  - Wire, mines, or lights near the beach landing site.
  - Alert status of units near the beach landing site.
  - Offshore platforms and anchorages that may interfere with the route.
  - Capability to reinforce the area of the beach landing site.
  - Proper cache of craft, as required.

DUTIES DURING ASSAULT

The rifle squad leader will —

- Lead the squad from the landing craft or amphibious vehicle.
- Gain contact with the platoon commander.
- Continue to estimate the situation.
- Revise the current plan or develop a new plan based on the current estimate of the situation.
- Inform the platoon commander of the squad's location, situation, planned action, casualties, and ammunition status.

Helicopterborne Operations

In addition to the general duties prescribed on page 2-1, the rifle squad leader is responsible for performing the following actions during helicopterborne operations.

TRAINING DUTIES

The rifle squad leader will —

- Assist the platoon commander in the conduct of training by supervising the squad in —
  - Embarkation and debarkation procedures.
  - Conduct in flight.
  - Preparation of manifest tags.
  - Safety precautions.
  - Emergency procedures.
  - Use of emergency equipment.
- Know the duties of a heliteam leader, as described in appendix C.

PLANNING DUTIES

The rifle squad leader will —

- Make a preliminary estimate of the situation.
- Conduct map and aerial photograph reconnaissance.

- Coordinate with adjacent squad leaders.
- Formulate a tentative plan of attack to include —
  - Heliteam organization.
  - Scheme of maneuver.
    - Clearing squad sector of landing site.
    - Movement to objective.
    - Seizure of objective.
  - Fire support.
- Submit the tentative plan of attack to the platoon commander.
- Brief the members of the squad on the mission and the commander's intent two levels up.
- Orient the squad to physical aspects of the landing site, its shape, size, and available cover.
- Complete the plan, issue the order, and supervise.

DUTIES IN THE ASSEMBLY AREA

The rifle squad leader will —

- Assemble the squad and ensure that it is properly equipped.
- Supervise the preparation of manifest tags.
- Carry out the duties of a heliteam or assistant heliteam leader.
- If a heliteam leader, embark the squad on order.

DUTIES DURING INITIAL GROUND ACTION

The rifle squad leader will —

- Establish tactical control of the squad.
- Continue an estimate of the situation.
- Revise current plans or develop new plans based on changes of the estimate of the situation.
- Carry out the assigned mission.
- Inform the platoon commander of squad location, estimate of the situation, and planned action.

Offensive Combat

In addition to the general duties prescribed on page 2-1, the rifle squad leader is responsible for the following actions during offensive combat.

MOVEMENT TO CONTACT — FOOT MARCH

Squad as Point of Advance Party

The rifle squad leader will —

- Conduct map and/or aerial photograph reconnaissance of the march route, with emphasis on start, release and checkpoints, obstacles along the route, and likely ambush sites.
- Include the following specific details in the march order:

- Initial squad formation.
- Assignment of a sector of observation to each fire team.
- Route and rate of march.
- Location and identifying features of control points.
- Security measures during halts.
- Accountability of personnel and equipment during all halts.

■ Follow the assigned route at the prescribed rate of march.

■ Conduct continuous reconnaissance to the front and immediate flanks of the march route.

■ Investigate likely ambush sites.

■ Report all enemy sighted.

■ Engage the enemy in order to —
- Ensure the unimpeded movement of the main body.
- Destroy him.
- Fix him by fire to cover the remainder of the advance party.

■ Report contact with the enemy, to include action taken, enemy location, disposition, and strength.

Squad as Flank Guard

The rifle squad leader will —

■ Conduct map and/or aerial photograph reconnaissance, with emphasis on avenues of approach to the march route and key terrain features dominating avenues of approach to the march route.

- In the march order, include specific details about the assignment of a sector of observation to each fire team and designation of the initial squad formation.

- Clear key terrain features assigned.

- Search other areas likely to conceal the enemy or provide him with good observation of the march column.

- Maintain contact with connecting elements.

- Report all enemy sighted.

- Engage the enemy, as necessary, in order to prevent exposure of the march column, protect the flank guard, or force disclosure of his positions, strength, and weapons.

- Report contact with the enemy, to include action taken, enemy location, disposition, and strength.

- Resist enemy attack until ordered to withdraw.

Squad as Rear Point

The rifle squad leader will —

- Conduct map and/or aerial photograph reconnaissance with emphasis on terrain that affords delaying positions.

- In the march order, include specific details about the assignment of a sector of observation to each fire team, designation of the inital squad formation, security measures during halts, and the employment of obstacles.

- Follow the march route at the prescribed distance from the rear party.

- Conduct continuous observation to the rear and immediate flanks of the march route.

- Select successive delaying positions.

- Withdraw elements of point by bounds or alternate bounds utilizing successive delaying positions.

- Report all enemy sighted.

- Conduct delaying actions when enemy action threatens to interfere with the march.

- Report contact with the enemy, to include action taken, enemy location, disposition, and strength.

Squad as an Element of a Blocking Position

The rifle squad leader will —

- Organize the assigned position.

- Conduct a reconnaissance of the route(s) of withdrawal.

- In the march order, include specific details about the assignment of a position and a sector of fire to each fire team, designation of sectors of observation, and assignment of route(s) of withdrawal.

- Report all enemy sighted.

- Engage the enemy, as necessary, and report action taken, enemy location, disposition, and strength.
- Withdraw on order.

Squad as Connecting Group

The rifle squad leader will —

- Maintain contact between march units.
- Designate squad formation.
- Assign a sector of observation to each fire team.
- Ensure rapid and accurate transmission of messages between units.

Squad as Element of Support or Main Body

The rifle squad leader will —

- Conduct map and/or aerial photograph reconnaissance.
- In the march order, include the following specific details:
  - Assignment of a sector of ground observation to each fire team.
  - Assignment of air sentinels, as directed.
  - March formation.
  - March distances to be maintained between individuals.
- Maintain march discipline.

- Ensure dispersion and unit security during halts.

MOVEMENT TO CONTACT — MECHANIZED MARCH

In addition to duties prescribed in the foot march paragraphs above, the following considerations apply to security missions assigned for a mechanized or motorized march. The rifle squad leader will —

- Utilize observation and reconnaissance by fire.
- Advance vehicles by bounds or alternate bounds when acting as point or rear point.
- Move vehicles off roads and utilize available cover and concealment during halts.

DUTIES IN THE ASSEMBLY AREA

The rifle squad leader will —

- Assign an area to each fire team.
- Establish security, as directed.
- Supervise actions taken to prepare or improve cover.
- Exercise continuous camouflage discipline, to include the following:
  - Removal of excess soil from position.
  - Proper use and timely replacement of natural camouflage materials.
  - Disposal of trash.

- Control of individual movement to avoid creating visible paths.
- Supervise the care and cleaning of weapons and equipment.
- Enforce light and noise discipline.
- Ensure the correct use of challenge and password.
- Enforce field sanitation measures.
- Afford equal opportunity for periods of rest consistent with security measures and actions to prepare for the attack.
- Supervise the segregation of equipment not required.
- Supervise the drawing and distribution of ammunition, pyrotechnics, rations, water, and special equipment.
- Report at the designated time and place to receive the platoon commander's orders.
- Conduct troop leading steps. (See appendix A.)
- Supervise the squad in specialized training and/or rehearsal.

DAYLIGHT ATTACK

On receipt of the platoon commander's order, the rifle squad leader will —

- Take maps, notebook, and pencil, ensure complete understanding of the squad mission, and arrange a time and place for detailed coordination with adjacent and supporting unit leaders.
- Begin planning:

- Allocate time for both personal and fire team leader's reconnaissance and planning, as well as squad movement forward from the assembly area and/or deployment.
- Using METT-T, make a preliminary estimate of the situation based on the mission, commander's intent, content of the platoon commander's order, and a map reconnaissance conducted during the platoon commander's orientation.
- Formulate a tentative plan of attack.

■ Arrange for —

- Movement of the squad forward from the assembly area, to include where, when, and how.
- A reconnaissance route and schedule to facilitate the prearranged meeting with adjacent and supporting unit leaders for coordination.

■ Make reconnaissance:

- Select a vantage point from which to orient fire team leaders, and a covered position nearby from which to issue the order.
- Determine enemy locations, strengths, and dispositions.
- Determine the following:
  - Attack position.
  - Line of departure.
  - Tentative assault position.
  - Key terrain.
  - Obstacles which may hinder or delay movement in the avenues of approach.
  - Cover and concealment.
- As the *platoon base of fire element* determine the following:

- Fire team's position with respect to the assigned target(s) or target area.
- Observation and fields of fire.
- Displacement route forward.
  - Effect coordination in accordance with the prearranged schedule.
- Complete the plan:
  - Complete an estimate of the situation.
  - As a *maneuver unit of the platoon*—
    - Determine initial squad formation, when not previously designated, based on METT-T.
    - Designate a base fire team.
    - Select the attack position.
    - Select the assault position and tentative final coordination line when the squad is the assault element.
    - Plan for breaching, crossing, or bypassing known obstacles.
    - Provide for additional security by employing scouting elements and assigning overlapping sectors of observation.
    - Designate a defensive position for each fire team on the objectives.
  - As the *platoon base of fire element*—
    - Designate a position and assign targets for each fire team.
    - Provide for protection of crew-served weapons employed in the platoon base of fire.
    - Consider the prescribed elements of fire control.
    - Determine a displacement route.
- Issue the order:

- Assemble subordinate unit leaders at the selected vantage point.
- Orient subordinate unit leaders, and ensure a thorough understanding of the orientation.
- Utilize the standard order form. (See appendix A.)
- Ensure a thorough understanding of the order.

■ Ensure preparedness for the attack.
■ Conduct the attack:

- As a *maneuver element of the platoon*—
  - Deploy the squad into initial attack formation prior to crossing the line of departure (LD).
  - Ensure the squad crosses the LD at the designated time.
  - Continue an estimate of the situation throughout the attack, and revise the plan as necessary through the use of fragmentary orders.
  - Maintain contact with the platoon commander.
  - Deploy fire teams into final assault formation upon reaching the assault position.
  - Ensure the commencement of the assault on the prearranged signal.
  - Ensure initiation of the signal for ceasing or shifting supporting fire, when appropriate.
  - Maintain momentum of the assault through the assigned objective.
  - Conduct pursuit by fire.
  - Report all enemy sighted.

- As the *platoon base of fire element*—
  - Assign sectors of fire and specific targets.

- Issue fire commands.
- Commence fire on order, signal, or at a designated time.
- Establish and maintain fire superiority.
- Maintain fire discipline.
- Cease or shift fires, as appropriate.
- Displace forward on order.

■ Reorganize:

- Assign a defensive position and sector of fire for each fire team.

- Reorganize promptly to reestablish subordinate chains of command and replace key billets made vacant by casualties.

- Redistribute ammunition.

- Provide for evacuation of casualties.

- Submit a casualty and ammunition status report to the platoon commander.

- In accordance with the assigned mission, either prepare to continue the attack or continue organization of the ground for defense.

NIGHT ATTACK

In the nonilluminated night attack, the following special considerations are integrated with the procedures prescribed for the daylight attack on page 2-15. The rifle squad leader will —

- Complete a plan:
  - Plan and conduct reconnaissance, as directed.
    - Exercise security precautions relative to reconnaissance parties in accordance with the platoon commander's instruction.
    - Locate a tentative squad release point.
    - Locate the assigned portion of the probable line of deployment (PLD) and objective.
    - Locate prominent terrain features to guide movement and assist in the identification of control points.
  - Coordinate with adjacent squad leaders concerning contacts between squads in the movement forward, unit contact on the PLD, and unit contact in consolidation.
  - Select the base fire team for movement forward, deployment on PLD, and the assault. Include specific instructions for guiding on adjacent squads during movement.
  - Determine a position for each fire team within the column based on the sequence of deployment(s) on the PLD.
  - Assign security missions to subordinate units, as directed.
  - Designate distances and intervals, as directed.
  - Plan for continuous movement through the squad release point.

- Provide for all-round squad security forward of the squad release point.
- Provide for detailed actions on discovery.

■ Prepare for the attack:

- Brief the entire squad on details of the operation.
- Participate in platoon rehearsals with particular attention to troop familiarity concerning —
  - Flare discipline.
  - Individual conduct, to include movement, maintaining distances and intervals, and light and noise discipline.
  - Security measures.
  - Signals.
  - Actions on discovery.
  - Actions after crossing the PLD.
  - Actions on the objective.
- Supervise troop preparations to include —
  - Implementation of individual camouflage.
  - Silencing equipment and clothing.
  - Removing or dulling shiny items.
  - Segregating equipment not required for the attack.
  - Issuing ammunition.
  - Checking weapons.

■ Conduct the attack:

- If an advance party, guide on the base squad. The base squad will maintain the direction and rate of advance.
- Exercise strict noise, light, and flare discipline throughout movement to the PLD.

- Ensure unit security forward of the squad release point.
- Upon discovery by the enemy, take the following actions, as directed by the platoon commander:
  - Deploy the squad, as necessary.
  - Advance by fire and movement to the PLD, as necessary.
- Eliminate enemy elements on the assigned portion of the PLD, if required.
- Rejoin elements of the patrol at the PLD, if applicable.
- Ensure deployment of squad on the PLD, and report readiness to the platoon commander.
- On the assault signal, commence assault fire and aggressive movement forward.
- On order, move the squad forward from the PLD silently, utilize assault formation, and maintain line and troop intervals.
- Assault through the assigned portion of the objective to the limit prescribed by the platoon commander.
- Conduct consolidation.

MECHANIZED INFANTRY ATTACK

In the mechanized infantry attack, the rifle squad is the base unit and will be mounted with combat support personnel in one assault amphibious vehicle (AAV). The following special considerations are integrated with the procedures prescribed for the daylight attack on page 2-15. The rifle squad leader will —
- Supervise the tactical loading of the AAV:

- The AAV will contain 13-25 personnel depending on the situation.

- Tactical integrity is maintained whenever possible.

- The senior maneuver unit leader embarked will serve as the vehicle commander.

  - The vehicle commander will direct the action of the vehicle in tactical situations. The vehicle commander must also be aware of the vehicle's capabilities and limitations regarding the terrain to be traversed.
  - The senior crewman will direct the action of the vehicle in administrative situations.

- Coordinate with the AAV crew chief, to include security measures during extended halts, communications during movement, and communications when dismounted.

- Determine the scheme of maneuver after dismounting, to include the dismount location, actions at dismount positions, and a plan that provides security for tanks and AAVs upon dismounting.

ATTACK OF FORTIFIED AREAS

In the attack of fortified areas, the following special considerations are integrated with the procedures prescribed for the daylight attack on page 2-15. The rifle squad leader will —

- Conduct a detailed reconnaissance with team leaders:
  - Locate the assigned emplacement and determine the number of embrasures, entrances, exits, air vents, types of weapons

within the placement, and the location and extent of defending troops providing small arms fire.

- Locate positions of —
  - Supporting emplacements, to include those in adjacent zones of action.
  - Supporting enemy infantry entrenchments.
  - Natural and artificial obstacles which will affect the squad attack.
  - Surfaces and gaps in enemy defenses within the zone of action.
- Determine the best avenues of approach consistent with the plan of attack.
- Select the assault position.
- Select a base of fire position that will allow the base of fire element to cover the advance of the assaulting units, shift fires rather than cease fires during the assault, or support adjacent units as prescribed in the platoon order attack.
- Select routes to the base of fire position and tentative assault position, and select a displacement route for the base of fire.

■ Formulate a tentative plan of attack based on the assigned mission, the mission of the adjacent unit, reconnaissance, recommendations of attached team leaders, and the fire support plan of the platoon and higher units.

■ Coordinate with —
- Appropriate supporting unit leaders to ensure they can support the tentative scheme of maneuver.

- Adjacent unit leaders with respect to the mutual support required or prescribed. Include targets to be engaged, sequence of engagement, and signals for commencing, ceasing, and/or shifting of fires.

- Complete the plan of attack:
  - Organize the squad into base of fire and assault elements.
  - If machine gun and assault teams are attached to the squad, assign them to the base of fire or assault element, as appropriate.
  - Provide for —
    - Breaching of minefields and wire obstacles when not accomplished by higher units. Plan the use of demolitions, bangalore torpedos, indirect fire, mats or boards, and probing.
    - A thorough search of the emplacement, adjoining troop shelters, and trenchworks.
    - Elimination of the enemy within and around the assigned emplacement.
    - Protection of crew-served weapons personnel.
    - Implementation of mutual support with adjacent units.
    - Easily recognizable coordinating signals between the base of fire, assault, and adjacent units, to include pyrotechniques, whistle, arm-and-hand signals, and radio.
  - Ensure that squad members receive instruction in the use of demolitions and crew-served weapons.
  - Conduct a rehearsal to check the attack sequence, timing, signals, and coordinated action with adjacent and supporting units.

ATTACK OF URBAN TERRAIN

In the attack of urban terrain, the following special considerations are integrated with the procedures for the daylight attack on page 2-15. The rifle squad leader will —

- Include in the estimate of the situation military aspects peculiar to the type of built-up area under attack.

- Conduct a detailed reconnaissance in order to —
  - Determine the relative position of assigned objectives.
  - Locate key buildings and/or key terrain within the squad's zone of action.
  - Locate and determine the best entrances into assigned buildings.
  - Locate killing zone positions for the support force.

- Formulate a plan of attack to include —
  - Employing standard techniques for thorough clearing of assigned objectives.
  - Coordinating mutual support with the other attacking squad(s).
  - Ensuring mutual support between fire teams during the advance.
  - Designating killing zones for the support force.
  - Designating a route of advance that minimizes or avoids movement in streets or open areas and does not mask killing zone fires.

- Clearing the entire squad zone of action.
- Employing the assigned marking code.

■ Ensure the squad has the necessary special equipment, to include toggle ropes, ladder(s), grappling hooks, satchel charges, and AT-4s/shoulder-launched multipurpose assault weapons (SMAWs).

■ Coordinate signals, to include pyrotechnical, arm-and-hand, whistle/other audio, and electronic.

■ Draw extra grenades and ammunition.

■ Conduct a rehearsal and/or review of house-to-house fighting techniques.

RIVER-CROSSING OPERATIONS

In river-crossing operations in an assault amphibious vehicle (AAV), the following special considerations are integrated with the procedures prescribed for the daylight attack on page 2-15. The rifle squad leader will —

■ Coordinate with the supporting AAV crew chief regarding the loading of vehicles, to include rehearsals, action in the event of vehicular casualty afloat, and action in the event of vehicular failure to negotiate the bank at the landing site.

■ Conduct a thorough briefing of fire team leaders.

■ Conduct rehearsals, as directed.

Defensive Combat

In addition to the general duties described on page 2-1, the rifle squad leader is responsible for the following actions during defensive combat.

SQUAD OF FRONTLINE PLATOON

On receipt of the platoon commander's order, the rifle squad leader will —

- Take maps, notebooks, and pencil, ensure a complete understanding of the squad mission, and arrange a time and place for detailed coordination with adjacent and supporting unit leaders.
- Begin planning:
  - Allocate time for —
    - Personal reconnaissance and planning.
    - Fire team leaders' reconnaissance and planning.
    - Movement of the squad to the defensive position.
    - Organization of the ground.
    - Preparation of the squad defensive fire plan sketch.
  - Using METT-T, make a preliminary estimate of the situation based on the content of the platoon commander's order, map reconnaissance, and the visual reconnaissance made with the platoon commander during the orientation.
- Arrange for —

- Movement of the squad to the defensive position, to include where, when, and how.
- A reconnaissance route and schedule to facilitate the prearranged meeting with adjacent and supporting unit leaders for coordination.

■ Make reconnaissance:

- Locate limits of the squad's defensive position.
- Locate limits of the squad's sector of fire.
- Select a vantage point from which to orient and issue the squad order.
- Evaluate the terrain considering OCOKA.
- Select the position and sector of fire for each fire team based on terrain analysis and the assigned mission. Positions and sectors should provide for coverage of the entire squad fire, mutual support between adjacent fire teams, and protection for crew-served weapons within the squad position.
- Determine the principal direction of fires (PDFs) for automatic rifles and grenade launchers based on the following considerations:
  - Coverage of enemy avenues of approach.
  - Protection of crew-served weapons.
  - Supplementation to the fires of crew-served weapons.
  - Coverage of obstacles.
  - Coverage of dead space in machine gun final protective lines (FPLs).

- Select your own position which provides for the best observation of the squad sector, control of the subordinate unit, and contact with the platoon commander.
- Locate the assigned supplementary position and select fire team supplementary positions therein.
- Locate assigned listening and sentinel posts, and select the best covered and concealed routes thereto.
- Coordinate, as planned, to ensure mutual support with adjacent units and protection of crew-served weapons.

■ Complete the plan:

- Assign a defensive mission to each fire team to include —
  - Position and sector of fire.
  - PDF for automatic rifles and grenade launchers.
  - Supplementary position and sector of fire.
  - Fire team responsibility for local security, protection of crew-served weapons, and obstacle construction.

- Plan coordinating instructions to include —
  - Priority of work, to include post security, position of automatic weapons, clearance of fields of fire, construction of obstacles/entrenchment, preparation of supplementary positions, and continuous improvement of camouflage.
  - Employment of limiting sector/PDF stakes, elevation and deflection stakes, and assignment of a forward limit.
  - Squad security measures.
  - Plans for fire control, including a final protective fire signal.

- Alert procedures for ground, air, and nuclear, biological, and chemical (NBC) attacks (see appendix G).
- Night security measures, to include movement, light and noise discipline, and challenge and password.

- Incorporate logistic considerations, including ammunition, food, water, and the location of corpsmen and the battalion aid station.

- Incorporate a signal and communication means for conduct of defense providing for —

    - Control of close defensive and final protective fires.
    - Contact with higher, adjacent, supporting, and subordinate leaders.
    - Warning of ground, armor, air, and NBC attack.
    - Location of the squad leader.
    - Location of the platoon command post (CP)/observation post (OP).
    - Location of the company CP/OP.

- Issue the order:

    - Issue the order from a vantage point.

    - Orient subordinates thoroughly to include —

        - Squad position and sector of fire.
        - Likely avenues of approach.
        - Targets and final protective fires.
        - Obstacles.

    - Walk the ground with subordinates, as necessary, to point out —

        - Specific location and responsibilities of each fire team.

- Sector of fire for each fire team.
- Location and PDF for each automatic rifle and grenade launcher.
- Locations of obstacles to be constructed.
- Location of FPL or PDF of each crew-served weapon in or near the squad position.

■ Supervise the following:

- Organization of the ground for establishment of security, as directed, location and construction of individual positions, and preparation of supplementary positions.

- Organization of fires to include —
  - Position and assignment of PDFs for automatic rifles and grenade launchers.
  - Integration of squad fires with supporting fires and the fires of adjacent units.
  - Assignment of individual sectors of fire.

- Construction of obstacles.
- Continuous improvement of camouflage.
- Distribution of supplies.

■ Submit a squad fire plan sketch to include —

- Fire team primary and supplementary positions.
- Sector of fire of each fire team.
- Location and PDF of each automatic rifle.
- Location and PDF or FPL for each crew-served weapon in the squad position.

- Location and PDF of each fire team leader.
- Terrain features, and estimated distances thereto, necessary for orientation of the sketch.
- Location of the squad leader.

■ Conduct the defense:

- Notify the platoon commander of enemy activity.
- Cover the withdrawal of local security.
- Fire close defensive fires, as planned.
- Maintain fire discipline and control.
- Fire final protective fires on signal.
- Defend the squad position by fire and close combat.
- Shift fire to cover gaps caused by casualties.
- Shift to supplementary positions on order.
- Inform the platoon commander of the situation at all times, to include penetrations, crew-served weapons out of action within or near position, and movement to supplementary positions when so ordered.
- When the enemy is destroyed or repelled —
  - Cease final protective fires on signal.
  - Pursue by fire until targets cease to exist.
  - Reorganize.
  - Redistribute ammunition.
  - Evacuate casualties.

- Submit a situation report, to include enemy situation, casualties, ammunition status, prisoners, documents, and significant material.

- Evacuate prisoners of war.

SQUAD IN THE SECURITY AREA

In the organization of a security force, the following special considerations are integrated with the procedures prescribed for squads of frontline platoons on page 2-28. The rifle squad leader will —

- Coordinate with adjacent security force commanders concerning position, patrol routes between positions, and mutually supporting fires.

- Conduct reconnaissance:
  - Select a position for each fire team which provides long-range observation, long-range fires across the entire security position, and mutual support within the security area.
  - Locate patrol routes and contact points assigned by the platoon commander.

- Determine a fire plan:
  - Plan long-range fires to delay an enemy advance.
  - Plan to cover the withdrawal of the covering force.
  - Provide for mutual fire support with adjacent squads.

- Establish security measures, to include sentinels, listening posts, patrols between squads, and warning devices.

- Plan for the withdrawal of the outguard using procedures prescribed for daylight withdrawals on page 2-42, as appropriate.
- Complete the plan:
  - Patrol, as directed.
  - Engage the enemy at maximum ranges, maintain pressure, and avoid close combat.
  - Report contact with the enemy.
  - Withdraw on order

SQUAD IN THE DEFENSE OF URBAN TERRAIN

In the defense of urban terrain, the following special considerations are integrated with the procedures prescribed for the squad of a frontline platoon on page 2-28. The rifle squad leader will —

- Conduct reconnaissance:
  - Locate building(s) assigned.
  - Select positions for each fire team in the assigned building.
  - Locate positions which provide for ground level, overhead, and subsurface security.
- Assign each fire team a building or portion of a building to defend.
- Assign principal directions of fire (PDFs) to automatic riflemen down streets and alleys.

- Establish close-in protection for crew-served weapons located in the assigned sector.

- Barricade, boobytrap, and plan fires on unoccupied buildings in the sector, as directed.

- Prepare to defend occupied buildings by —
  - Barricading windows, doors, and other openings.
  - Removing drain pipes, vines, and projections which can assist the enemy in gaining outside access to the upper floors or roofs.
  - Sandbagging individual positions on upper floors for protection.
  - Constructing individual barricades in rooms for protection.

    NOTE: Be careful to prepare barricades that do not interfere with the movement of friendly forces.

- Report the location of boobytraps to the platoon commander.

Relief Operations

In addition to the general duties prescribed on page 2-1, the rifle squad leader has the responsibility to perform the following actions during retrograde operations.

RELIEF IN PLACE

Responsibilities of the Incoming Rifle Squad Leader

- Provide liaison personnel, as directed.
- Conduct daylight reconnaissance with emphasis on —
  - Defensive position and sector of fire of the outgoing squad.
  - Location and missions of crew-served weapons within the outgoing squad position.
  - Position, principal direction of fire (PDF), and sector of fire for each automatic rifle and grenade launcher in the outgoing squad.
  - Sector of fire for each fire team in the outgoing squad.
  - Location of the platoon command post (CP)/observation post (OP).
  - Terrain.
  - Location of the squad release point for incoming squads, and an assembly area for outgoing squads.
  - Route from the release point to the assigned position.
  - Location at which to meet the guide from the outgoing unit.
  - Establishment of a sequence of relief by the fire team.
- Arrange for daylight reconnaissance by fire team leaders.
- Conduct a detailed briefing of fire team leaders.
- Minimize movement on the forward edge of the battle area (FEBA).

- Notify the platoon commander when relief is complete.

Responsibilities of the Outgoing Rifle Squad Leader

- Receive liaison personnel from the incoming squad.
- Provide guides for the incoming squad, as directed.
- Assist the incoming squad leader on reconnaissance.
- Conduct your own reconnaissance with emphasis on the withdrawal route and assembly area.
- Dispatch fire teams to the assembly area as they are relieved.

PASSAGE OF LINES

In the passage of lines, the following special considerations are integrated with the procedures prescribed for the daylight attack (page 2-15) or night attack (page 2-20), as appropriate.

Responsibilities of the Attacking Rifle Squad Leader

- Meet with the squad leader of the squad in contact.
- Conduct daylight reconnaissance with emphasis on —
  - Assembly area.
  - Route to the line of departure.
  - Area(s) of passage, as directed by the platoon commander.
  - Gaps or lanes in minefields and wire obstacles.

- Location of local security elements through which squads will pass.
- Location at which to meet a guide from the unit in contact.
- Enemy situation, known/suspected location, recent activity.

Responsibilities of the Rifle Squad Leader of the Unit in Contact

- Brief the attacking squad leader on the enemy situation and area of operations.
- Assist the attacking squad leader on his reconnaissance.
- Provides guides, as directed.
- Provide administrative, logistic, and fire support, as directed.

Retrograde Operations

In addition to the general duties prescribed on page 2-1, the rifle squad leader is responsibile for performing the following actions during retrograde operations.

NIGHT WITHDRAWAL

Responsibilities of the Rifle Squad Leader of the Unit Initially Withdrawing

- Issue a warning order to provide for maximum use of daylight for preparation and reconnaissance and give reasons for movement.
- Prepare a plan to include —
  - Conducting personal reconnaissance with emphasis on location of the squad assembly areas(s) and route(s) to the assembly area(s).
  - Providing guides, as directed.
  - Providing security patrols, as directed.
  - Conducting a thorough briefing of fire team leaders.
  - When withdrawing through a friendly unit, ensuring that fire team leaders know mutual recognition signals, routes of withdrawal, and area(s) of passage.
- Conduct the action:
  - Assist the detachment left in contact in manning positions.
  - On order, commence withdrawal to the squad assembly area.
  - Destroy supplies and equipment, as directed.
  - Ensure rapid, quiet movement during withdrawal.
  - When withdrawing through a friendly unit, pass through rapidly and notify the commander when the squad has effected passage.

Responsibilities of the Rifle Squad Leader of the Detachment Left in Contact

- Issue a warning order to provide for maximum use of daylight for preparation and reconnaissance, and to give reasons for movement.

- Prepare a plan to include —
  - Reporting to the commander of the detachments left in contact, usually the company executive officer, for additional instruction.
  - Conducting personal reconnaissance with emphasis on selection of positions to be occupied, location of the company assembly area, and selection of route(s) to the company assembly area.
  - Coordinating with leaders of crew-served weapons units concerning attachments to the squad, close-in protection of weapons not attached, using existing wire communications, and conducting a thorough briefing of fire team leaders and attached weapons unit leaders.

- Conduct the action:
  - On order, occupy previously selected positions. Automatic rifles will remain in position until directed to withdraw. Riflemen withdraw to successive covering positions or the platoon assembly area, as planned.
  - Destroy supplies and equipment, as directed.
  - When withdrawing through a friendly unit, pass through rapidly and notify the platoon commander when the squad has effected passage.

DAYLIGHT WITHDRAWAL

In the daylight withdrawal of the squad as an element of the reserve platoon, the following special considerations are integrated with procedures prescribed for the squad as an element of the frontline platoon on page 2-28. The rifle squad leader will —

- Coordinate with frontline unit leaders, as directed, concerning administrative and logistic support requirements of frontline units and fire support requirements.

- Formulate a detailed plan of covering fires in support of the withdrawal in consonance with prior coordination agreements.

DELAYING ACTION

In the delaying action, the following special considerations are integrated with the procedures prescribed for the area defense (page 2-28) and withdrawal (page 2-39). The rifle squad leader will —

- Prepare a plan to include —
  - Conducting a personal reconnaissance with emphasis on —
    - Location of assigned initial delaying position(s).
    - Location of assigned subsequent delaying position(s).
    - Availability of observation and fields of fire from the topographical crest.
    - Routes of withdrawal and rally points.
  - Organizing the ground.
  - Engaging the enemy by fire at maximum range.

- Conduct the action:
  - Engage the enemy by fire at maximum range.
  - Avoid close combat.
  - Execute the planned withdrawal on order.

Mine Warfare

In addition to the general duties prescribed on page 2-1, the rifle squad leader is responsible for performing the following actions during mine warfare.

HASTY PROTECTIVE MINEFIELD INSTALLATION

During installation of a minefield, the rifle squad leader will —

- Organize the squad to emplace mines, as directed by the platoon commander.

- Know the arming/disarming procedure and the method of employment for each type of mine used, to include fuzing, arming, burying, camouflaging, and safety.

- Know all major features and characteristics for a hasty protective minefield.

- After mines are emplaced and armed, collect and verify the count of mine safety pins/clips.

- Turn in mine safety pins/clips to the platoon commander.

RIFLE SQUAD

- Ensure that all squad members know the exact location of the minefield(s).

MINEFIELD BREACHING

During deliberate breaching of a minefield, the rifle squad leader will —

- Organize the squad into a breach party, assigning specific responsibilities to each member.
- Inspect the squad to ensure members have the required equipment, and question them on their assignments and specific responsibilities.
- Establish a position which best controls the breach party at all times.
- Maintain direction and work in a cleared area. Keep the squad at least 100 paces from an adjacent breach party.
- Relieve personnel periodically, or as needed.
- Maintain communications with the platoon commander.

Mob and Riot Control

In addition to the general duties prescribed on page 2-1, the rifle squad leader is responsible for performing the following actions during mob and riot control. The rifle squad leader will —

- Make recommendations to the platoon commander concerning the best use of available training time based on the proficiency of individuals in riot control positions, use of the field protective mask, and basic duties and functions.

- Conduct training:
  - Ensure a thorough understanding of the mission stated alert plans.
  - Supervise training in individual and unit actions in riot control formations, as directed.
  - Supervise training in the preparation and use of available riot control agents and apparatus, as directed.
  - Supervise individual and unit execution of contingency plans during rehearsals.
  - Recommend individuals to be trained as selected marksmen.
  - Supervise training in the establishment and defense of roadblocks and street barricades.

- Carry out the action:
  - Issue the warning order.
  - Form the unit, as directed.
  - Construct and defend roadblocks/street barricades, as directed.
  - On order, control and supervise execution of riot control formations.

- On order, be prepared to employ riot control agents or apparatus, selected marksmen, the firepower of the squad, or combat formations, tactics, and firepower.

CHAPTER 3

FIRE TEAM

The **mission** of the **fire team** is to locate, close with, and destroy the enemy by fire and movement, or repel the enemy's assault by fire and close combat.

This chapter discusses the duties of the **fire team leader**

General Duties

In addition to the procedures prescribed for all troop leaders in appendix A, the fire team leader will —

- Conduct tactical training of the fire team, as directed by the squad leader.

- Control the tactical employment of the fire team in combat and training operations through the use of appropriate troop leading procedures.

- Supervise and control the safeguarding and economical use of supplies and equipment of the fire team.

- Supervise first echelon maintenance of weapons and equipment through frequent inspection.

- Ensure each team member is familiar with the squad, platoon, and company missions, in addition to knowing the team mission.

- Know the procedures for requesting and conducting air and artillery strikes, as well as the procedures for requesting helicopter MEDEVACs.

Amphibious Operations

In addition to the general duties prescribed on page 3-1, the fire team leader is responsible for performing the following actions during amphibious operations.

PRE-EMBARKATION DUTIES

The fire team leader will —

- Ensure the fire team attends all periods of training and instruction.
- Supervise preparation of the fire team for pre-embarkation inspections.
- Supervise the fire team in marking/tagging of weapons, equipment, and baggage for embarkation.
- Assemble the fire team in proper uniform at the designated time for embarkation.

DUTIES ABOARD SHIP

The fire team leader will —

- Assign individual bunks and supervise the stowage of gear.
- Ensure the fire team attends all briefings and periods of instruction.
- Supervise the policing of the fire team berthing area, and report discrepancies in ship's facilities to the squad leader.
- Enforce applicable ship's regulations.
- Ensure care, cleaning, and security of weapons.
- Instruct the men on their specific duties afloat and ashore.

DUTIES DURING SHIP-TO-SHORE MOVEMENT

The fire team leader will —

- Assemble the fire team in the boat team assembly area.
- Inspect the fire team for proper rigging of weapons and equipment prior to debarkation.
- Supervise the positioning of the fire team in landing craft, amphibious vehicle, or rigid raiding craft (RRC)/combat rubber raiding craft (CRRC).

DUTIES DURING ASSAULT

The fire team leader will —

- Lead the fire team from the landing craft or amphibious vehicle.
- Establish tactical control of the fire team.

- Carry out the fire team mission.
- Establish contact with the squad leader.
- Employ M203.
- Control squad automatic weapons fires.

Helicopterborne Operations

In addition to the general duties prescribed on page 3-1, the fire team leader is responsible for the following actions during helicopterborne operations.

TRAINING DUTIES

The fire team leader will —

- Ensure the fire team attends all periods of instruction.
- Assist the squad leader, as directed.
- Ensure the fire team understands —
    - Embarkation and debarkation procedures.
    - Conduct in flight.
    - Preparation of manifest tags.
    - Safety precautions.
    - Emergency procedures.
    - Use of emergency equipment.

- Know the duties of the heliteam leader as described in appendix C.

DUTIES IN THE ASSEMBLY AND HOLDING AREAS

The assembly area may also be the holding area. The fire team leader will —

- Assemble the fire team and ensure that it is properly equipped.
- Supervise preparation of manifest tags.
- Carry out the duties of assistant heliteam leader, as described in appendix C.
- Embark the fire team on order.

DUTIES DURING INITIAL GROUND ACTION

The fire team leader will —

- Establish tactical control of the fire team.
- Establish contact with the squad leader.
- Carry out the assigned mission.

Offensive Combat

In addition to the general duties prescribed on page 3-1, the fire team leader is responsible for the following actions during offensive combat.

MOVEMENT TO CONTACT

Fire Team as Part of Point, Rear Point, or Flank Security

The fire team leader will —

- Select or alter fire team formations, as influenced by the mission, terrain, speed of movement and control, unit security, and enemy action.
- Assign a sector of observation to each individual.
- Conduct continuous reconnaissance/surveillance of the assigned area (i.e., front, rear, or flank).
- Search assigned areas rapidly, aggressively, and thoroughly.
- Investigate likely ambush sites. Reconnaissance by fire may be used.
- Mark all boobytraps.
- Report all enemy sighted.
- Engage enemy within range.
- Report contact with the enemy, to include action taken, enemy location, disposition, and strength.
- Ensure unimpeded movement of the main body.

Fire Team as an Element of a Blocking Position

The fire team leader will —

- Organize the position:
    - Establish contact with the unit on flanks.
    - Ensure assigned sectors of fire overlap with units on flanks.
    - Locate a route of withdrawal.
    - Assign a position and sector of fire to each individual.
    - Provide for continuous observation of the fire team sector.
    - Report all enemy sighted.
    - Engage the enemy, as necessary, and report action taken, enemy location, disposition, and strength.
- Withdraw on order.

Fire Team as Connecting Group

The fire team leader will —

- Maintain contact between march units.
- Designate fire team formation.
- Assign a sector of observation to each individual.
- Ensure rapid and accurate transmission of messages.

Fire Team as Element of Support or Main Body

The fire team leader will —

- Assign a sector of observation to each individual.
- Maintain march discipline.
- Ensure dispersion and unit security during halts.

DUTIES IN THE ASSEMBLY AREA

The fire team leader will —

- Assign each individual a position within the fire team area.
- Establish security, as directed.
- Supervise detailed actions taken to prepare or improve cover.
- Exercise continuous camouflage discipline to include —
  - Use and timely replacement of natural camouflage material.
  - Disposal of trash.
  - Control of individual movement to avoid creating visible paths.
- Closely supervise the care and cleaning of weapons and equipment.
- Enforce light and noise discipline.
- Ensure the fire team understands the correct use of challenge and password.
- Enforce field sanitation measures.

- Segregate equipment not required.
- Inspect each individual to ensure prescribed loads of ammunition, rations, water, and special equipment.
- Report at the designated time and place to receive the squad leader's order.
- Conduct applicable troop leading steps (see appendix A).
- Supervise the fire team in specialized training and/or rehearsals.

DAYLIGHT ATTACK

On receipt of the squad leader's order, the fire team leader will —

- Take notebook and pencil, and ensure a complete understanding of the fire team mission.
- Begin planning:
  - Allocate time for personal reconnaissance and planning, as well as fire team movement forward from the assembly area and/or deployment.
  - Using METT-T, make a preliminary estimate of the situation.
  - Formulate a tentative plan of attack.
- Arrange for —
  - Reconnaissance and coordination with adjacent fire team leaders and supporting unit leaders, as necessary.
- Make reconnaissance:
  - Determine enemy location, strength, and disposition.

- As a *maneuver unit,* determine the following:
  - Line of departure (LD).
  - Assault position.
  - Objective(s) and intermediate objectives, if used.
  - Obstacles.
  - Squad avenues of approach.

- As a *base of fire element,* determine the following:
  - Assigned fire team position.
  - Position for each individual with good observation and fields of fire.
  - Route of displacement forward.

- Complete the plan:
  - Using METT-T, complete an estimate of the situation.
  - As a *maneuver unit*—
    - Determine initial combat formation when not designated, based on terrain, enemy situation, security, control, flexibility, and speed.
    - Assign each individual a sector of observation.
    - Plan for breaching, crossing, or bypassing obstacles, as directed.
    - Designate individual defensive positions on the objective.
  - As a *base of fire element*—
    - Designate individual positions and targets.
    - Provide protection of crew-served weapons, as directed.
    - Consider the prescribed elements of fire control.
    - Plan for displacement.

- Issue the order:
  - Assemble the fire team in a covered position.
  - Orient the fire team, and ensure a thorough understanding of the orientation.
  - Utilize the standard order form (see appendix A).
  - Ensure a thorough understanding of the order.
  - Inspect each man to ensure preparedness for the attack, with emphasis on ammunition, rations, water, individual camouflage, and special equipment.
- Conduct the attack:
  - As a *maneuver unit*—
    - Deploy the fire team into initial attack formation prior to crossing the line of departure (LD).
    - Maintain contact with the squad leader at all times.
    - Conduct fire and movement, as directed by the squad leader.
    - Deploy into final assault formation upon reaching the assault position.
    - Commence the assault on prearranged signals.
    - Maintain assault formation and momentum of the assault through the assigned portion of the objective.
    - Conduct pursuit by fire.
  - As a *base of fire element*—
    - Assign sectors of fire and specific targets.
    - Issue fire commands.
    - Commence fire on order, signal, or at a designated time.
    - Establish and maintain fire superiority.

- Maintain fire discipline.
- Cease or shift fires, as directed.
- Displace forward on order.

■ Reorganize:

- Assign each individual a position and sector of fire.
- Reorganize and replace key billets made vacant by casualties.
- Redistribute ammunition.
- Notify the squad leader of ammunition status and casualties.

NIGHT ATTACK

In the nonilluminated night attack, the following special considerations are integrated with the procedures prescribed for the daylight attack on page 3-9. The fire team leader will —

■ Prepare a plan:

- Conduct reconnaissance, as directed:
  - Implement security precautions as required by the findings of the squad leader's reconnaissance.
  - Locate terrain features and control points designated in the squad leader's order.
- Coordinate with adjacent fire team leaders concerning —
  - Contact between fire teams in the movement forward.
  - Unit contact on the probable line of deployment (PLD) and on the objective.
  - Guiding on base fire team.

- Assign individuals to security missions.
- Designate individual distances and intervals, as directed.

■ Prepare for the attack:

- Participate in the squad rehearsal with particular attention to troop familiarity concerning —
    - Actions on the objective.
    - Actions after crossing the PLD.
    - Signals.
    - Flare discipline.
    - Radio discipline.

- Supervise troop preparations to include —
    - Individual camouflage.
    - Silencing equipment and clothing.
    - Removing or dulling shiny items.
    - Segregating equipment not required for the attack.
    - Issuing ammunition.
    - Checking weapons.

■ Conduct the attack:

- Advance, guiding on base fire team. The base fire team will maintain the direction and rate of advance.

- Exercise strict noise, light, and flare discipline throughout movement to the PLD.

- Ensure deployment of the fire team on the PLD and report readiness to the squad leader.

- On order, move the fire team forward from the PLD and maintain intervals.

- Assault through the assigned portion of objective to the limit of advance.

■ Assume a defensive posture or continue the attack in accordance with the platoon mission.

MECHANIZED INFANTRY ATTACK

The fire team is part of the squad mounted in assault amphibious vehicles (AAVs) during the mechanized attack. In the mechanized infantry attack, the following special considerations are integrated with the procedures prescribed for the daylight attack on page 3-9. The fire team leader will —

■ Know the squad leader's duties, as outlined on page 2-22.

■ For mechanized infantry dismounted attacks —

- Ensure individuals know and utilize the prescribed visual signals.

- Reconnoiter all suspected areas by fire if observation is limited, ensuring that the word is passed throughout the chain of command of the intention to fire.

- Brief the fire team concerning safety precautions, as appropriate, to include movement in front or abreast of a tank or light armored vehicle (LAV) that is firing. With the 120mm main gun on the M1A1 tank, there are more precautions to consider. The over-pressure from the 120mm can kill a Marine found within a 90 degree arc extending from the muzzle of the gun tube out to 200 meters. From 200 meters to 1,000 meters, dismounted Marines must be aware of the discarding sabot hazard. The 25mm APDS-T round creates a hazardous situation for exposed personnel due to thrown pieces of the sabot. The 25mm APDS-T danger zone extends from the muzzle, out to at least 100 meters, and about 17 degrees left and right of the muzzle.

ATTACK OF FORTIFIED AREAS

In the attack of fortified areas, the following special considerations are integrated with the procedures prescribed for the daylight attack on page 3-9.

Fire Team as Base of Fire Element

The fire team leader will —

- Plan for positive control of fires in support of assaulting units and adjacent units, as directed.
- Provide for protection of attached and supporting units in the vicinity of the base of fire position.
- Plan for replacing crew members of attached or supporting weapons in the event of casualties.

Fire Team as an Assault Unit

The fire team leader will —

- Provide protection for supporting elements moving with the fire team.

- Plan for breaching obstacles.

- Prepare/employ demolitions when assaulting with demolitions.

- Upon seizure of the objective, ensure a thorough search of the emplacement and adjoining trenches, and provide support by fire, as directed.

ATTACK OF URBAN TERRAIN

In the attack of built-up areas, the following special considerations are integrated with the procedures for the daylight attack on page 3-9.

Fire Team as an Assault Unit

The fire team leader will —

- Organize the fire team into —
  - A clearing team to make initial entry into rooms being cleared and clear each room in building.
  - A covering team to remain outside rooms being cleared and cover the clearing team.
- Clear buildings, or portions of buildings, in the squad's assigned zone of action.
  - With entry from the uppermost level, clear the floor of entry and work down.

- With entry on the middle floor, clear the floor of entry, move to the top deck, and clear down.
- With entry on the ground level, use demolitions, shoulder-launched multipurpose assault weapons (SMAWs), or other supporting weapons to blast an entry passage, clear the floor, move to the top deck, and clear down.
- Clear each room, including the attic and basement.
- Ensure there is coordinated action between the clearing and covering teams by loud and clear voice commands.
- Mark all boobytraps.
- Mark buildings, as prescribed, when cleared.

Fire Team as an Element of Support or Security Unit

The fire team leader will —

- Protect the advance of assault units.
- Provide killing zone fires.
- Displace on order.

RIVER-CROSSING OPERATIONS

The considerations of the fire team leader in conducting river-crossing operations are the same as the procedures prescribed for the daylight attack on page 3-9.

Defensive Combat

In addition to the general duties prescribed on page 3-1, the fire team leader is responsible for performing the following actions during defensive combat.

FIRE TEAM OF FRONTLINE SQUAD

On receipt of the squad leader's order, the fire team leader will —

- Take notebook and pencil, and ensure a complete understanding of the fire team mission.
- Begin planning:
  - Allocate available time for personal reconnaissance and planning and organization of the fire team position.
  - Prepare for the defense.
- Arrange for reconnaisance.
- Make reconnaissance:
  - Evaluate the terrain considering OCOKA.
  - Locate the limits of the fire team defensive positions.
  - Locate the lateral limits of the fire team sector of fire.
  - Based on the assigned mission and terrain analysis, select a position and sector of fire for each individual which will provide for —
    - Coverage of the entire fire team sector by fire.

- Overlapping fires.
- One or two-man positions, as directed.
- Close-in protection for crew-served weapons, as directed.

• Select your own position which provides for —

- Best observation of the fire team sector.
- Control of M249 automatic weapon fires.
- Contact with the squad leader.
- Effective employment of the M203.

• Locate the assigned fire team supplementary position, and select individual positions therein.

■ Complete the plan:

• Assign each individual a primary position and sector of fire.

• Assign each individual a supplementary position and sector of fire, as directed.

• Plan coordinating instructions to include —

- The priority of work prescribed by the squad leader.
- Employment of limiting and principal direction of fire (PDF) stakes.
- Details of squad security measures which affect the fire team.
- Plans for fire control, including final protective fire (FPF) signals.
- Alert procedures, as directed by the squad leader.
- Night security measures, to include movement, light and noise discipline, challenge and password, location of and personnel assignment to sentinel posts (SPs)/listening posts (LPs), and the time, point of departure, point of return, and composition of all patrols.

- Location of the platoon corpsmen and battalion aid station.
- Incorporate a signal and communication means providing for —
  - Commencing and ceasing fires.
  - Firing final protective fires.
  - Warning of ground, armor, air, and nuclear, biological, and chemical (NBC) attack.
  - Location of the fire team leader.
  - Location of the squad leader.
  - Location of the platoon commander.

- Issue the order:
  - Orient the fire team thoroughly, to include the fire team position and sector of fire, likely avenues of approach, targets, concentrations, and obstacles.
  - Walk the ground with the fire team to point out —
    - Specific position for each individual.
    - Sector of fire for each individual.
    - PDF for automatic rifleman and the fire team leader/grenadier.
    - Location of the PDF or final protective line (FPL) of each crew-served weapon located within or near the fire team position.
- Supervise the following:
  - Clearance of fields of fire.
  - Construction of individual positions.
  - Employment of limiting and PDF stakes.

- Construction of obstacles.
- Improvement of camouflage.

■ Conduct the defense:
  - Notify the squad leader of enemy activity.
  - Cover the withdrawal of local security, as directed.
  - Fire close defensive fires, as planned.
  - Maintain fire discipline and control.
  - Fire final protective fires on signal.
  - Defend the fire team position by fire and close combat.
  - Shift fire, as directed.
  - Shift to the supplementary position on order.
  - Inform the squad leader of the situation.
  - When the enemy is destroyed or repelled —
    - Cease final protective fires on signal.
    - Pursue by fire until targets cease to exist.
    - Reorganize.
    - Redistribute ammunition.
    - Evacuate casualties.
    - Inform the squad leader of ammunition status, casualties, prisoners, captured documents, and material.

FIRE TEAM AS PART OF A SECURITY ELEMENT

In the organization of the fire team as a part of a security element, the considerations of the fire team leader are generally the same as the procedures described for the fire team of the frontline squad on page 3-18; however, close combat is avoided and withdrawals are conducted on order.

FIRE TEAM IN THE DEFENSE OF URBAN TERRAIN

In the defense of urban terrain, the following special considerations are integrated with the procedures prescribed for the fire team of the frontline squad on page 3-18. The fire team leader will —

- Prepare the building to be occupied:
  - Barricade windows, doors, and other openings.
  - Remove drain pipes, vines, and projections which can assist the enemy in gaining outside access to upper floors or roofs.
  - Sandbag individual positions in upper floors for protection from fires from below.
  - Construct individual barricades in rooms for protection.
- Report the location of boobytraps to the squad leader.

Relief Operations

In addition to the general duties prescribed on page 3-1, the fire team, leader is responsible for performing the following actions during relief operations.

RELIEF IN PLACE

Responsibilities of the Incoming Fire Team Leader

- Conduct daylight reconnaissance with emphasis on —
  - Defensive position and the sector of fire of the outgoing fire team.
  - Position, principal directions of fire (PDFs), and sectors of fire of each man.
  - Squad leader position.
  - Terrain.
  - Location of the squad release point.
  - Route to position.
- Move the fire team to position on order..
- Brief each man concerning his position, PDF, and sector of fire.
- Permit time for each man to be oriented by the man he is relieving.
- Minimize movement on the forward edge of battle area (FEBA).

Responsibilities of the Outgoing Fire Team Leader

- Assist the incoming fire team leader on his reconnaissance.
- Conduct your own reconnaissance with emphasis on the withdrawal route and assembly area.
- Permit time for each man to orient the man relieving him.
- Move the fire team to the squad assembly area on order.

PASSAGE OF LINES

The fire team leader of a unit executing a passage of lines carries out the procedures prescribed for the daylight attack (page 3-9) or night attack (page 3-12), as appropriate. The fire team leader further ensures that the passage of lines is effected in accordance with the squad leader's attack order.

The fire team leader of the unit being passed through provides administrative, logistic, and fire support, as directed.

Retrograde Operations

In addition to the general duties prescribed on page 3-1, the fire team leader is responsible for performing the following actions during retrograde operations.

NIGHT WITHDRAWAL

Fire Team as Part of the Squad Initially Withdrawing

The fire team leader will —

- Inform the men of the reason for movement.
- Prepare a plan to include —
  - Conducting personal reconnaissance, if the situation permits, with emphasis on location of the squad assembly area and the route(s) to the assembly area.
  - Conducting a thorough briefing of the fire team.
- Conduct the plan:
  - Withdraw the fire team to the squad assembly area on order.
  - Ensure rapid, quiet movement during withdrawal.

Fire Team as Part of the Squad Left in Contact

The fire team leader will —

- Inform the men of the reason for movement.
- Prepare a plan to include —
  - Conducting reconnaissance, with emphasis on the locations of positions to be occupied and the company assembly area.
  - Conducting a thorough briefing of the fire team.
- Conduct the plan:

- Occupy the previously located position on order.
- Maintain the impression of normal activity.
- Use existing wire communications.
- On order, destroy wire communications.
- On order, commence withdrawal.
- Ensure rapid, quiet movement during withdrawal.

DAYLIGHT WITHDRAWAL

Fire Team as Element of Frontline Squad

The fire team leader will —

- Inform the men of the reason for movement.
- Prepare a plan to include —
  - Conducting reconnaissance, with emphasis on withdrawal routes, and locations of rallying points and covering positions.
  - Occupation of covering positions, as directed.
  - Conducting a thorough briefing of the fire team.
- Conduct the plan:
  - Direct the automatic riflemen to remain in position.
  - Withdraw the remainder of the fire team, as directed on order.
  - Direct the automatic riflemen to withdraw.

Fire Team Employed as a Part of the Reserve Platoon

The fire team leader will —

- Plan for the withdrawal, as outlined in the procedures for daylight withdrawal (fire team as element of frontline squad) on page 3-26.
- Brief the men concerning the zones/routes of withdrawal of the frontline units.
- Provide covering fires, as directed.
- Withdraw on order.

DELAYING ACTION

In the delaying action, the following special considerations are integrated with the procedures prescribed for the area defense (page 3-18) and withdrawal (page 3-24). The fire team leader will —

- Organize a position on or near the topographical crest, unless otherwise directed.
- Engage the enemy by fire at maximum range.
- Execute the planned withdrawal.

Mob And Riot Control

In addition to the general duties prescribed on page 3-1, the fire team leader is responsible for performing the following actions during mob and riot control. The fire team leader will —

- Conduct training:
  - Supervise training on individual and fire team actions in riot control formations, as directed, to include riot control positions, use of field protective masks, and basic riot control duties and functions.
  - Supervise training in the preparation and use of available riot control agents and apparatus, as directed.
  - Supervise individual action during rehearsals of contingency plans.
  - Recommend individuals to be trained as selected marksmen.
  - Supervise training in the establishment and defense of roadblocks and street barricades, as directed.
- Carry out the action:
  - Form the unit, as directed.
  - Construct and defend roadblocks and street barricades, as directed.
  - On order, be prepared to employ riot control agents or apparatus, selected marksmen, combat formations, tactics, and firepower.

CHAPTER 4

WEAPONS PLATOON
Platoon Commander

The **mission** of the **weapons platoon** is to provide the Marine rifle company supporting fires for maneuvering or defending elements of the company, close-in antitank protection, assault fires against fortified areas and obstacles, and a limited demolition capability to destroy and reduce fortified positions and obstacles.

This chapter discusses the duties of the **weapons platoon commander.**

General Duties

In addition to the procedures prescribed for all troop leaders in appendix A, the weapons platoon commander will —

- Plan and conduct technical and tactical training of the weapons platoon in accordance with the company training directives.

- Make recommendations for, and direct the tactical employment of, the weapons platoon in training and combat operations through appropriate use of troop leading procedures.

- Conduct reconnaissance, as directed, to assist the company commander specifically in —
  - Determination of suitable targets for fire missions.

- Determination of the most effective method of employment of the weapons platoon in support of the company scheme of maneuver.
- Selection of firing position areas for organic crew-served weapons and those attached to the company.
- Formulation of the company fire support plan.

▪ Coordinate the tactical employment of the weapons platoon with other supporting weapons, to include prompt displacements as necessary to accomplish the mission.

▪ Ensure that all feasible means of communications are utilized to establish and maintain fire control of weapons.

▪ Revise estimates of the situation continually during the conduct of operations in order to more effectively accomplish fire support missions.

▪ Direct and supervise the location and construction of unit positions, tactical wire, ground obstacles, and continuous camouflaging of positions and equipment.

▪ Ensure the timely requisitioning, distributing, safeguarding, and economical use of supplies and equipment.

▪ Ensure first echelon maintenance of weapons and equipment through frequent inspection.

▪ Supervise the administrative functions of the platoon, including records relating to personnel, training, combat casualties, and other directed functions.

▪ Enhance combat efficiency, discipline, and morale by applying standard health, comfort, and welfare measures consistent with tactical considerations.

The weapons platoon commander is assisted in his duties by the **weapons platoon sergeant** who will —

- Assist in all aspects of supervision and control of the platoon.
- Perform such administrative and logistics functions as the weapons platoon commander may direct to include —
  - Supervision and maintenance of gun books.
  - Responsibility for supply and timely resupply in combat.
  - Maintenance of the platoon casualty records and medical evacuation.
- Assume command in the absence of the weapons platoon commander.

Amphibious Operations

In addition to the general duties prescribed on page 4-1, the weapons platoon commander is responsible for performing the following actions during amphibious operations.

PRE-EMBARKATION DUTIES

The weapons platoon commander will —

- Conduct training:
  - Supervise instruction for the individual in —

- Ground combat skills, with emphasis on technical training of crew-served weapon crews.
- Rigging of individual weapons, equipment, and life preservers for debarkation.
- Lashing and lowering techniques for crew-served weapons and equipment.
- Actions while boated.
- Procedures for landing in assault amphibious vehicle (AAV), landing craft, or rigid raiding craft (RRC)/combat rubber raiding craft (CRRC).
- Procedures for emergency abandonment of AAV, landing craft, or RRC/CRRC.
- Familiarization firing of all individual and crew-served weapons and setting battlesights.

• Direct and control training for the unit in —

- The tactical employment of the weapons platoon in the amphibious assault and subsequent operations ashore.
- The basic procedures and control involved in the ship-to-shore movement.
- Naval customs and troop life aboard ship.

• Train the weapons platoon in the purpose, functioning, and organization of the boat team. Emphasize the duties and responsibilities of deck and boat loaders, and boat handlers.

■ Prepare a plan:

• Make a detailed study of available planning aids. These planning aids include maps, aerial photographs, shoreline photographs, area and objective studies, intelligence reports, and summaries.

• Make a preliminary estimate of the situation.

- Submit recommendations concerning weapons platoon employment based on the company commander's intent and concept of operations, and the preliminary estimate of the situation.

- Ensure preparedness of weapons, clothing, and equipment for the operation.

- Check service records to verify the following data is contained therein:
  - Emergency data forms.
  - Eligibility for combat.
  - ID/Geneva Convention Cards (DD 2MC).
  - Servicemen's Group Life Insurance.
  - Wills and powers of attorney.

- Ensure that lashing lines are obtained prior to embarkation.

- Ensure complete preparedness for embarkation, as directed.

DUTIES ABOARD SHIP

The weapons platoon commander will —

- Inspect the platoon berthing space to determine the adequacy and serviceability of bunks, life preservers, lockers, heads, weapons locks, and armory.

- Assign bunks to subordinate units by blocks in order to facilitate rapid debarkation.

- Brief the platoon concerning —
  - Actions to be taken during ship's drill.

- Applicable ship's regulations.
- Musters.
- Messing.
- Use of ship's facilities, to include the barber shop, library, movies, ship's store, and laundry.
- Assignments to the ship's platoon, if applicable.

■ Inspect the following daily and correct or report deficiencies:
- Personnel.
- Weapons and equipment for serviceability and maintenance.
- Troop compartment to ensure —
    - Decks and bulkheads are clean.
    - Bunks are made and properly secured.
    - Equipment is properly stowed and secured.
    - Weapons are secure.
    - Ventilation systems are functioning and unobstructed.
    - Head facilities and scuttlebutts are clean and operable.
    - Ships equipment is properly maintained.
    - Availability and serviceability of troop compartment cleaning gear.

■ Direct and supervise training to include —
- Physical conditioning and exercise.
- Military subjects pertinent to the operation.
- Maintenance of weapons and equipment.
- Test firing of machine guns.
- Machine gun, mortar, and assault section technical training.

- Conduct operational planning:
  - Brief NCOs concerning —
    - Company mission, battalion mission, and intents of the commanders two levels up.
    - Scheduled rehearsals.
    - Debarkation procedures.
    - Ship-to-shore movement.
  - Complete a tentative plan.
- Issue the order, and ensure a thorough understanding by utilizing mockups, sketches, maps, aerial photographs, and question and answer techniques.

DUTIES DURING SHIP-TO-SHORE MOVEMENT

The weapons platoon commander will carry out the duties of the boat team commander, as described in appendix B, when appropriate.

DUTIES DURING ASSAULT

The weapons platoon commander will —

- Continue estimates of the situation.
- Assist the company commander in implementing the plan of attack by revising the fire support plan, as necessary.

Helicopterborne Operations

In addition to the general duties prescribed on page 4-1, the weapons platoon commander is responsible for the following actions during helicopterborne operations.

TRAINING DUTIES

The weapons platoon commander will —

- Conduct individual training in —
  - Embarkation and debarkation procedures, to include stowage of crew-served weapons, ammunition, and equipment.
  - Conduct in flight.
  - Preparation of manifest tags.
  - Safety precautions.
  - Emergency procedures.
  - Use of emergency equipment.
- Conduct platoon training in —
  - Heliteam organization and duties of leaders (see appendix C).
  - Actions in the assembly and holding areas, pickup zone, loading point, and landing site/zone.
  - Initial ground orientation, to include use of compass azimuth and terrain features.
- Conduct drills related to initial ground action and readily identifiable terrain features, reestablishment of tactical control, and use of compass azimuth for orientation.

PLANNING DUTIES

The weapons platoon commander will —

- Using METT-T, make a preliminary estimate of the situation.
- Conduct map, aerial photograph, or aerial reconnaissance.
- Submit the recommended plan for employment of the platoon to the company commander.
- Coordinate with supported unit commanders, to include arrangements for attachments.
- Designate a heliteam and assistant heliteam commander, when appropriate.
- Submit a heliteam loading plan, when directed, based on —
  - Plan of attack.
  - Type and number of helicopters assigned.
  - Tactical integrity of subordinate units.
  - Dispersion of crew-served weapons and key personnel.
- Brief the members of the platoon on the company mission and commander's intent.
- Complete the plan and issue the order.
- Supervise.

DUTIES IN THE ASSEMBLY AREA

The weapons platoon commander will —

- Assemble the platoon and ensure that it is properly equipped.
- Conduct a final briefing and orientation of subordinate unit leaders.
- Ensure the correct preparation of manifest tags.
- Direct the platoon to report to assigned heliteams.
- Carry out the duties of the heliteam commander, if so assigned.

DUTIES DURING INITIAL GROUND ACTION

The weapons platoon commander will continue estimates of the situation in order to assist the company commander in implementing the plan of attack. Revise the company fire support plan, as necessary.

Offensive Combat

In addition to the general duties prescribed on page 4-1, the weapons platoon commander is responsible for the following actions during offensive combat.

MOVEMENT TO CONTACT — FOOT MARCH

Platoon as Part of Support or Main Body

The weapons platoon commander will —

- Conduct map and/or aerial photograph reconnaissance with emphasis on all critical points along the march route.
- Include the following specific details in the march order:
  - Assignment of sectors of ground observation.
  - Assignment of air sentinels.
  - Designation of connecting files.
  - Formation of support or main body.
  - March distances to be maintained between units and individuals.
  - Route and rate of march.
  - Security measures during halts.
- Maintain march discipline.
- Ensure dispersion and unit security during halts.
- Be prepared to have elements assume security missions.

MOVEMENT TO CONTACT — MOTORIZED MARCH

In addition to the duties described in the foot march paragraph above, the following considerations apply to missions assigned for a motorized march. The weapons platoon commander will —
- Harden wheeled vehicles.
- Request additional radio communications.

- Provide for tactical integrity in vehicle assignments.

- Conduct reconnaissance by fire when mounted.

- Provide flank security by observation and reconnaissance by fire.

- Move vehicles off roads and utilize available cover and concealment during halts.

- Ensure that troops are properly trained and rehearsed in immediate action drills for convoy operations in near ambush, far ambush, and road blocked situations.

DUTIES IN THE ASSEMBLY AREA

The weapons platoon commander will —

- Assign each section an area to provide for dispersion, unit security, and concealment.

- Issue a warning order, to include time of attack, platoon mission, time and place for issuance of the attack order, and administrative preparation for the attack.

- Take action to prepare or improve available cover and concealment.

- Exercise continuous improvement of camouflage and other counterintelligence measures against ground and air observation. This should include —
    - Removal of excess soil from positions.
    - Use and timely replacement of natural camouflage material.
    - Movement control measures to avoid creating visible paths.

- Disposal of trash.
- Correct radio/telephone procedure.
- Correct use of challenge and password.
- Light and noise discipline.

- Ensure that weapons and equipment are clean and serviceable.
- Establish and maintain field sanitation measures.
- Provide for periods of rest to the maximum extent possible consistent with security measures and action to prepare for the attack.
- Designate a segregating area for unnecessary equipment.
- Direct the drawing and distribution of ammunition, pyrotechnics, rations, water, and special equipment.
- Report at the designated time and place to receive the company commander's order.
- Conduct troop leading steps as described in appendix A.
- Conduct specialized training and/or rehearsals.
- Conduct a final communications check.

DAYLIGHT ATTACK

The weapons platoon commander will accompany the company commander to receive the battalion attack order. Take a messenger, map, binoculars, notebook, and pencil, and leave the radio with the platoon.

On receipt of the battalion commander's attack order —

- Take notes with emphasis on the fire support available to the company.
- Effect coordination, as directed, concerning details of the battalion fire support plan.
- Assist the company commander in his reconnaissance concerning fire support planning, as directed, to include one of the following:
  - Planning separate reconnaissance.
    - Clarify the reconnaissance mission and the company tentative scheme of maneuver.
    - Prearrange a rendezvous with the company commander for submission of recommendations.
    - Allocate time for your own reconnaissance and planning.
    - Rendezvous with the company commander at the designated time and place.
  - Conducting a joint reconnaissance with the company commander.
- Begin planning:
  - Make a preliminary estimate and develop a tentative fire support plan considering —
    - Fire support available from nonorganic weapons.
    - Tentative scheme of maneuver for the company.
    - Allocation of available fires.
    - Methods of employment of organic crew-served weapons.

- Terrain.

• Conduct reconnaissance to determine —

  - Extent and location of reported and suspected enemy positions.
  - Probable effects of planned fires on enemy.
  - Location of key terrain features in the company zone of action and their probable influences on scheme(s) of maneuver and ability to deliver accurate fire.
  - Avenues of approach to these key terrain features.
  - Avenues of approach for enemy armor.
  - Positions, fields of fire, and targets for weapons.
  - Displacements required to maintain continuous fire support.

• Submit recommendations to the company commander at the appointed time and place to include —

  - Methods of employment of assault, machine gun, and mortar sections.
  - Supporting fires required.
  - Location of positions and targets.
  - Displacements.
  - Fire control means for coordination.
  - Consolidation of position areas and targets.

On receipt of the company commander's order —

- Take the platoon sergeant, a messenger, maps, binoculars, notebooks, and pencils.

- Arrange for a time and place for detailed coordination with supported unit commanders, to include general support fires available and the time and place to effect attachments.
- Continue planning:
  - Allocate time for further personal reconnaissance and planning, as required, as well as the subordinate commander's reconnaissance and planning, and movement of the platoon forward from the assembly area.
  - Using METT-T, continue an estimate of the situation based on the company plan of attack and reconnaissance.
- Arrange for —
  - Attachment of subordinate units, as directed.
  - Movement of the platoon forward from the assembly area.
  - A reconnaissance route and schedule to facilitate prearranged meetings with supported unit commanders for coordination, as required.
  - Participation of section leaders in reconnaissance, as required.
  - Time and tentative place to issue the order.
- Make further reconnaissance, as necessary, to include —
  - Selecting a concealed vantage point and covered position nearby from which to orient subordinate unit leaders and issue the order. (Notify section leaders of the time and place to receive the order.)
  - Determining the location and disposition of assigned targets not previously reconnoitered.

- Confirming targets and positions from which to deliver accurate fire.
- Determining safety limits for maneuvering units and other elements of fire control.
- Effecting coordination with supported unit commanders in accordance with the prearranged schedule considering employment of weapons in general support of the attack and follow-on mission (specified or implied).

■ Complete the plan:
- Receive recommendations from section leaders participating in the reconnaissance concerning weapons employment.
- Complete an estimate of the situation, to include defensive considerations after the attack and continuation of the attack.
- Assign position areas and specific targets for weapons based on the mission of the company (scheme of maneuver), observation, fields of fire, and the effective range of weapons.
- Prescribe fire control measures for each section to include —
  - Time or signal for opening fire, shifting fire, and ceasing fire.
  - Rate of fire.
  - Safety limits.
- Prescribe displacement instructions for each section to include —
  - Method of displacement.
  - Time of signal for displacement.
  - Route of displacement.
  - New position.

- Missions at displacement.
- Provide for security at all gun positions and during all unit movements.
- Ensure maximum use of camouflage.
- Designate the location of the platoon corpsman.
- Ensure that all pertinent extracts from the company commander's order are considered in completing plans.
- Prescribe the location and special control functions for the platoon sergeant.
- Determine your own position from which the control of fires can best be effected.

■ Issue the order:

- Orient subordinate unit leaders, and ensure a thorough understanding of the orientation.
- Utilize a standard order form (see appendix A).
- Ensure a thorough understanding of the order.

■ Supervise subordinate unit commander planning, effective detachments, and positioning of units.

■ Conduct the attack:

- Commence fire support at the prescribed time.
- Maintain fire control and coordination with the assistance of subordinate unit leaders.
- Continue the estimate of the situation throughout the attack.

- Recommend changes to the method of employment of the platoon, as appropriate.
- Coordinate displacement to ensure continuous fire support and accomplishment of consolidation missions.
- Maintain unit security during displacements.

■ Actions after displacement:

- Supervise execution of subordinate unit defensive missions. Adjust dispositions, as necessary.
- Coordinate with rifle unit commanders, as necessary, to ensure protection of crew-served weapons and support of their defensive positions.
- Expedite casualty and ammunition status reports from subordinates.
- Reorganize promptly to reestablish subordinate chains of command and replace key billets made vacant by casualties.
- Redistribute ammunition and replenish, if required.
- Evacuate casualties.
- Establish unit security at all gun positions.
- Report consolidation to the company commander to include —
  - Enemy situation.
  - Friendly casualties.
  - Ammunition status.
  - Information concerning prisoners of war, captured documents, and captured material.

- Recommendations concerning nonorganic fire support to augment weapons platoon fires.

• In accordance with the assigned mission, either prepare to support the continuation of the attack through issuance of fragmentary orders, or supervise the continued organization of the ground for defense.

NIGHT ATTACK

In the nonilluminated night attack, the following special considerations are integrated with the procedures prescribed for the daylight attack on page 4-14. The weapons platoon commander will —

- Plan and conduct reconnaissance to —

  • Coordinate with rifle platoon commanders on selection of the route to the objective.

  • Locate prominent terrain features to guide displacement to the objective.

    - Determine azimuths.
    - Determine the location of obstacles and measures to overcome them.
    - Number of guides required.

  • Plan for special measures to be taken for silencing equipment and clothing, preparing individual camouflage, and disposition of items not required for the attack.

- Prescribe control measures as necessary and in consonance with those prescribed by the company commander. These include —
  - Control points.
  - Flare discipline.
  - Individual conduct.
  - Action to be taken if discovered prior to reaching the probable line of deployment (PLD).
  - Movement forward from the PLD on order.
  - Commencement of assault fires.
  - Primary and alternate signal means to control movement and fire support.
- Plan a platoon rehearsal for a night attack.

■ Prepare for the attack:
  - Lay weapons on targets during daylight, if possible.
  - Brief the entire platoon on details of the operation.
  - Ensure that unit leaders of attached elements report to rifle platoon to receive the order.
  - Conduct a rehearsal with particular attention to troop familiarity concerning —
    - Flare discipline.
    - Individual conduct, to include movement, maintaining distances and intervals, light and noise discipline, and security measures.
  - Supervise troop preparations to include —
    - Individual camouflage.
    - Silencing equipment and clothing.
    - Removing or dulling shiny items.

- Segregating equipment not required for the attack.
- Issuing ammunition and pyrotechnics.
- Checking weapons.

■ Conduct the attack:

- Exercise strict noise, light, and flare discipline.
- Report readiness of the weapons platoon elements for the assault to the company commander.

OTHER OFFENSIVE OPERATIONS

The following special considerations are integrated with the procedures prescribed for the weapons platoon in the daylight attack (page 4-14). The weapons platoon commander is responsible for the following actions as appropriate for each type operation:

Platoon in the Mechanized Infantry Attack

Elements of the weapons platoon will be mounted with supported rifle squads in assault amphibious vehicles (AAVs). The following requires special consideration by the weapons platoon commander:

■ Conduct a rehearsal with supporting vehicles and embarked rifle unit(s) to include —

- Maintenance of tactical integrity, where possible.
- Mounting and dismounting procedures and locations.
- Actions on dismounting.
- Communications procedures, to include visual signals.

Dismounted Attacks

- Ensure the platoon is familiar with safety precautions, to include communication procedures and target acquisition procedures.

Platoon in the Attack of Fortified Areas

- Conduct a detailed reconnaissance to determine the location and extent of —
  - Individual emplacements to include —
    - Type of construction.
    - Number of embrasures.
    - Types of weapons and their fields of fire.
    - Entrances, exits, and air vents.
    - Location and number of defending troops providing supporting small arms fire.
  - Supporting fortifications in assigned and adjacent zones.
  - Underground fortifications.
  - Natural and artificial obstacles.
  - Strong and weak points in the enemy defense.
  - Positions for platoon elements.
- Develop a plan that provides for fires to support obstacle breaching operations and emplacement seizure.

Platoon in the Attack in Urban Terrain

- Conduct a detailed reconnaissance and make plans to —

  - Select streets and alleys that provide the best killing zones to support the attack.

  - Coordinate with supported units concerning signals for lifting, shifting, or ceasing of fires within killing zones.

  - Keep machine guns and rockets well forward for close fire support of assaulting units.

  - Use 60mm mortars to fire into defilade positions and provide illumination, as necessary.

River-Crossing Operations

- Conduct a rehearsal with supporting vehicles, if practicable, to include loading and unloading procedures, actions on unloading, and communication procedures.

Defensive Combat

In addition to the general duties prescribed on page 4-1, the weapons platoon commander is responsible for the following actions during defensive combat.

WEAPONS PLATOON IN THE DEFENSE

The weapons platoon commander will —

- Accompany the company commander to receive the battalion defense order. Take a messenger, map, binoculars, notebook, and pencil, and leave the radio with the platoon.

On receipt of the battalion commander's defense order —

- Take notes with emphasis on fire support available to the company. Effect coordination, as directed, concerning details of the battalion fire support plan.
- Assist the company commander in his reconnaissance, as directed, concerning fire support planning.
- Plan separate reconnaissance:
  - Clarify the reconnaissance mission to determine —
    - Prospective positioning of the rifle platoons.
    - Trace of the forward edge of battle area (FEBA).
    - General position areas for weapons.
    - General final protective lines (FPLs) for machine guns.
    - Avenues of approach to be covered by assault teams.
    - Final protective fires and targets.

- Prearrange a rendezvous with the company commander for submission of recommendations.
- Allocate time for your own reconnaissance and planning.
- Rendezvous with the company commander at the designated time and place.

■ Conduct a joint reconnaissance with the company commander.

■ Begin planning:

- Make a preliminary estimate and develop a tentative fire support plan considering —
    - Fire support available from nonorganic weapons.
    - Tentative defense plan for the company.
    - Allocation of available fires.
    - Employment of organic crew-served weapons.
    - Terrain.

- Make reconnaissance to determine —
    - Location of key terrain features in the the company area of responsibility.
    - Avenues of approach.
    - Positions for machine guns, to include primary and alternate positions, final protective line (FPL)/principal direction of fire (PDF), and supplementary positions, as directed.
    - Positions for assault squads or teams, to include covered hiding positions, primary and alternate positions, sector of responsibility, and supplementary positions, as directed.
    - Positions for mortar, to include primary and alternate, sectors of observation, and final protective fires (FPFs).

- Coordination of nonorganic supporting fires with organic fires.

• Submit recommendations to the company commander at the appointed time and place to include —

- Method of employment of assault and machine gun sections.
- Supporting fires required.
- Location of crew-served weapons positions (primary, alternate, and supplementary), PDF, FPLs, sector(s) of fire, and fire control means for coordination.

On receipt of the company commander's defense order—

■ Take the platoon sergeant, messenger, maps, binoculars, notebooks, and pencils, and arrange for a time and place for a detailed coordination with rifle platoon commanders.

■ Continue planning:

• Allocate time for —

- Further personal reconnaissance and planning, as required.
- Subordinate commander reconnaissance and planning.
- Movement of the platoon forward from the assembly area.
- Organization of the platoon defense area.

• Using METT-T, continue an estimate of the situation based on company plan of defense and reconnaissance.

■ Arrange for —

• Attachment of subordinate units, as directed.

• Movement of the platoon forward from the assembly area.

- A reconnaissance route and schedule to facilitate prearranged meetings with rifle platoon commanders for coordination, as required.
- Participation of section leaders in the reconnaissance, as required.
- A time and tentative place to issue the order.

■ Make further reconnaissance, as necessary, to include —

- Selecting a vantage point from which to orient subordinate unit leaders and issue the order. (Notify section leaders of the time and place to receive the order.)
- Confirming position areas, PDFs, FPLs, FPFs, and sectors of fire responsibility.
- Completing an analysis of the terrain within and adjacent to the assigned company defense and security areas, with emphasis on OCOKA.
- Effecting coordination with supported unit commanders in accordance with the prearranged schedule. The employment of weapons in the general support of the defense, and close-in protection for crew-served weapons should be considered.

■ Complete the plan:

- Receive recommendations concerning weapons employment from section leaders participating in the reconnaissance.
- Using METT-T, complete an estimate of the situation.
- Assign positions, specific FPLs, PDFs, FPFs, and sectors of fire for machine guns and mortars, as appropriate, as well as sectors of responsibility for assault teams based on the

mission of the company, observation, fields of fire, and the effective range of weapons.

- Prescribe fire control measures for each section to include —
  - Time or signal for commencing FPF, ceasing FPF, and certain prescribed teams or squads to engage targets of opportunity within the sector of fire.
  - Rate of fire.
  - Safety limits.
- Provide for security at all gun positions.
- Ensure the proper use of camouflage.
- Designate the location of the platoon corpsman.
- Ensure that all pertinent extracts from the company commander's order are considered in completing the plan.
- Prescribe the location and special control functions for the platoon sergeant.
- Determine your own position from which the control of fires can best be effected.

■ Issue the order:
  - Orient subordinate unit leaders, and ensure a thorough understanding of the orientation.
  - Utilize the standard order form (see appendix A).
  - Ensure a thorough understanding of the order.

■ Supervise —
  - Subordinate unit planning.

- Preparation and organization of the ground, with emphasis on security, weapons positioning, emplacement construction, camouflage, and communications (to include wire to squad positions, if possible).

■ Submit a fire plan sketch, to include positions, sector of fire/sector of responsibility for each unit, FPL/PDF for each machine gun, and location of FPFs and targets.

■ Conduct the defense:

- Notify the company commander of the enemy activity.
- Maintain fire discipline and control.
- On order or signal, fire final protective fires.
- Inform the company commander of the situation at all times making recommendations or changes in employment, as directed.
- When the enemy is repelled —
  - Cease final protective fires, as directed.
  - Maintain pursuit by fire until targets cease to exist.
  - Reorganize.
  - Redistribute ammunition.
  - Evacuate casualties.

WEAPONS PLATOON IN THE DEFENSE OF URBAN TERRAIN

In the defense of urban terrain, the following special considerations are integrated with the procedures prescribed for the platoon in defense. The weapons platoon commander will —

- Conduct reconnaissance:
  - Determine probable points at which falling debris may block machine gun final protective fires (FPFs).
  - Select machine gun positions on or as near ground level as observation and fields of fire allow.
  - Select one primary position and several alternate positions for each assault squad. Utilize rooftops and upper floors to provide better observation and fields of fire.
- Make recommendations to the company commander regarding the use of street barricades, mines, and other obstacles.
- Report the location of all boobytraps to the company commander.

Relief Operations

In addition to the general duties prescribed on page 4-1, the weapons platoon commander is responsible for the following actions during relief operations.

RELIEF IN PLACE

Mutual Considerations of Incoming and Outgoing Weapons Platoon Commanders

- Exchange information of the enemy situation and area of operation.
- Conduct detailed planning of the weapons exchange.
- Plan for the execution of a coordinated fire plan throughout the relief.
- Exchange information pertaining to the existing communications system.

Responsibilities of the Incoming Weapons Platoon Commander

- Attach weapons squads, as directed, to the incoming rifle platoon in whose areas their positions are planned.
- Make recommendations to the company commander relative to the extent of the weapons exchange.
- Study the company fire plan.
- Conduct a daylight reconnaissance to include —
  - Position, sector of fire, and final protective line (FPL)/ principal direction of fire (PDF) of each machine gun.
  - Determining dead space in the final protective fire (FPF).
  - Position, sector of fire, and PDF of each assault squad.
  - Alternate position, supplementary position, and mission for each weapon.
  - Determine the location of other existing supporting fires.

- Brief the section leaders and arrange for their reconnaissance.
- Supervise the weapons exchange, if applicable.
- Upon completion of relief, resume control of the weapons and employ them in accordance with the assigned mission.
- Make recommendations to the company commander for changing position or fire plan, if necessary.

Responsibilities of the Outgoing Weapons Platoon Commander

- Attach weapons squads, as directed, to outgoing rifle platoons in whose areas they are positioned.
- Assist the incoming weapons platoon commander with his reconnaissance.
- Supervise the exchange of weapons, if applicable.
- Move with the company commander to the company assembly area.
- Resume control of all weapons, unless otherwise directed.

PASSAGE OF LINES

In the passage of lines, the following special considerations are integrated into the procedures prescribed for the daylight attack (page 4-14) or night attack (page 4-20), as appropriate.

Responsibilities of the Attacking Weapons Platoon Commander

- Receive a briefing on the enemy situation and area of operations from the outgoing weapons platoon commander of the unit in contact.

- Conduct a daylight reconnaissance with emphasis on —
  - Platoon assembly area, if appropriate.
  - Route(s) to the line of departure (LD) or firing positions.
  - Area(s) of passage.
  - Gaps or lanes in minefields and wire obstacles.
  - Disposition of the weapons of the unit in contact.

- Make recommendations to the company commander for integrating fires of the company in contact into the fire support plan.

- Arrange for daylight reconnaissance by subordinate leaders.

Responsibilities of Weapons Platoon Commander of the Unit in Contact

- Brief the attacking commander on the enemy situation.
  - Assist the attacking commander with his reconnaissance.
  - Provide guides, as directed.
  - Provide fire support for the attack, as directed.

Retrograde Operations

In addition to the general duties prescribed on page 4-1, the weapons platoon commander is responsible for the following actions during retrograde operations.

WITHDRAWAL AND DELAYING ACTION

The weapons platoon commander will —

- Issue a warning order to provide for maximum use of daylight for preparation and reconnaissance, subordinate planning, and reasons for movement.
- Attach weapons squads to the platoon, as directed.
- When the company is moving to new defensive positions —
  - Relinquish control of the platoon to the platoon sergeant.

- Lead the company reconnaissance party to the new position.
- Conduct reconnaissance with emphasis on selecting platoon defense areas and selecting a position for each weapon.
- Direct the installation of wire communications.
- Post platoon guides to meet platoons and guide them into the new position.

■ Resume control of the weapons platoon when in new positions or in the company assembly area, as appropriate.

Mob And Riot Control

When engaged in mob and riot control operations, the weapons platoon will either be organized into a fourth rifle platoon or be assigned special missions.

When organized and employed as a rifle platoon, the weapons platoon commander will carry out the procedures prescribed for the rifle platoon commander during mob and riot control (page 1-76). The remaining members of the platoon segregate and protect the crew-served weapons in order that they are readily available for use should riot control techniques fail to quell the disturbance.

Special missions which may be assigned to the weapons platoon include the defense of vital installations, coverage and/or breaching of roadblocks and street barricades, and operations in urban terrain.

CHAPTER 5

WEAPONS PLATOON
Section Leader

The **mission** of the **section** is to provide supporting fires for maneuvering or defending elements of the rifle company.

This chapter discusses the duties of the **weapons platoon section leader.**

General Duties

In addition to the procedures prescribed for all troop leaders in appendix A, the weapons platoon section leader will —

- Plan and conduct technical and tactical training of the section, as directed by the weapons platoon commander.

- Through appropriate use of troop leading procedures, make recommendations for, and direct the tactical employment of, the section.

- Designate position areas, sectors of fire/responsibility, specific targets, and fire control measures for squads.

- Coordinate the employment of the section, or elements thereof, with rifle platoons and supporting units, as directed.

- Supervise the construction of squad positions, the installation of tactical wire, and the continuous improvement of camouflage of positions and equipment.

- Ensure that ammunition for the section is replenished, as required.

- Supervise first echelon maintenance of weapons and equipment through frequent inspection.

- Provide information for inclusion in platoon records and reports.

Amphibious Operations

In addition to the general duties prescribed on page 5-1, the weapons platoon section leader is responsible for performing the following actions during amphibious operations.

PRE-EMBARKATION DUTIES

The weapons platoon section leader will —

- Conduct training:
  - Ensure the section attends all instruction.
  - Assist the platoon commander in conducting and supervising individual, weapons, and unit training, as directed.
  - Instruct all NCOs on troop leading responsibilities in shipboard living and tactical operations ashore.

- Conduct inspections of weapons, clothing, and equipment to ensure preparedness for the operation and embarkation.

- Supervise the marking/tagging of weapons, equipment, and baggage for embarkation, as directed.

- Assemble the section in proper uniform at the designated time for embarkation.

DUTIES ABOARD SHIP

- Assign berthing areas and supervise the stowage of gear.

- Ensure the section attends all briefings and periods of instruction.

- Ensure the section area is in a good state of police through assignment of police details, close supervision, and frequent inspection.

- Hold physical musters, as directed.

- Enforce applicable ship regulations.

- Assist in conducting and supervising training to include —
  - Physical conditioning exercises.
  - Military subjects, stressing those which are important to the operation.
  - Maintenance of weapons and equipment.

- Supervise the security of individual weapons.

- Report all discrepancies in ship's facilities.

- Ensure the correct conduct and appearance of the section.

- Inspect berthing areas for proper policing and for equipment left behind prior to debarkation.

DUTIES DURING SHIP-TO-SHORE MOVEMENT

The weapons platoon section leader will carry out the duties of assistant boat team commander, as described in appendix B, if appropriate.

DUTIES DURING ASSAULT

- Assist the weapons platoon commander, as directed.
- Continue an estimate of the situation and make prompt recommendations of the most efficient employment of machine gun/assault/mortar squad fires in support of the mission.

Helicopterborne Operations

In addition to the general duties prescribed on page 5-1, the weapons platoon section leader is responsible for the following actions during helicopterborne operations.

TRAINING DUTIES

The weapons platoon section leader will —
- Assist the platoon commander in the conduct of training in —

- Embarkation and debarkation procedures (including the stowage of machine guns, rocket launchers, and ammunition).
- Actions during flight.
- Preparation and use of manifest tags.
- Safety precautions.
- Emergency procedures.
- Use of emergency equipment.

- Know the duties of the heliteam leader, as described in appendix C.
- Instruct all NCOs on troop leading responsibilities with respect to —
  - Heliteam organization.
  - Actions in the assembly and holding areas, pickup zone, loading point, and landing site/zone.
  - Initial ground orientation in the objective area by use of compass and terrain features.

PLANNING DUTIES

The weapons platoon section leader will —

- Make a preliminary estimate of the situation.
- Conduct map and aerial photograph reconnaissance.
- Coordinate with supported unit commanders.

- Formulate a tentative plan of employment and submit to the platoon commander.
- Complete the plan and issue the order.

DUTIES IN THE ASSEMBLY AREA

The weapons platoon section leader will —

- Assemble the section and ensure that it is properly equipped.
- Supervise the preparation of manifest tags.
- Carry out the duties of the heliteam or assistant heliteam leader, if applicable.

DUTIES DURING INITIAL GROUND ACTION

The weapons platoon section leader will —

- Assist the weapons platoon commander, as directed.
- Continue estimates of the situation and make prompt recommendations to him on the most efficient employment of the section in support of the mission.
- Promptly establish control of attached squads, when directed.
- Assist attached squads in effecting prompt resupply of ammunition.
- Keep the weapons platoon commander informed of the situation.

Offensive Combat

In addition to the general duties prescribed on page 5-1, the weapons platoon section leader is responsible for the following actions during offensive combat.

MOVEMENT TO CONTACT — FOOT MARCH

The weapons platoon section leader will —

- Conduct map and/or aerial photograph reconnaissance of the march route.
- Include the following specific details in the march order:
  - Assignment of a sector of observation to each squad.
  - Assignment of air sentinels, as directed.
  - March information.
  - March distances to be maintained.
- Maintain march discipline.
- Ensure dispersion and unit security during halts.

MOVEMENT TO CONTACT — MOTORIZED MARCH

In addition to duties described in the foot march paragraph above, the following considerations apply to security missions assigned for a motorized march. The weapons platoon section leader will —

- Utilize observation and reconnaissance by fire.
- Provide flank security by observation and reconnaissance by fire.
- Move vehicles off roads and utilize available cover and concealment during halts.

DUTIES IN THE ASSEMBLY AREA

The weapons platoon section leader will —

- Assign an area for each squad.
- Establish security, as directed.
- Supervise actions taken to prepare or improve cover.
- Exercise continuous camouflage discipline to include —
  - Removal of excess soil from position.
  - Use and timely replacement of natural camouflage materials.
  - Disposal of trash.
  - Control of individual movement to avoid creating visible paths.
- Supervise the care and cleaning of weapons and equipment.
- Enforce light and noise discipline.
- Ensure the correct use of challenge and password.
- Enforce field sanitation measures.
- Afford equal opportunity for periods of rest consistent with security measures and action to prepare for attack.

- Supervise the segregating of unnecessary equipment.

- Supervise the drawing and distribution of ammunition, rations, water, and special equipment.

- Report at the designated time and place to receive the platoon commander's order.

- Direct and supervise detachments, as prescribed:
  - Notify involved squads of the time and place to join the supported unit.
  - Inspect weapons and equipment prior to detachment.

- Conduct troop leading steps (see appendix A).

- Supervise the section in specialized training and/or rehearsal.

DAYLIGHT ATTACK

On receipt of the company attack order by the platoon commander —

- Assist the platoon commander in reconnaissance, as directed.

- Accompany the platoon commander on his reconnaissance mission, or conduct separate reconnaissance, as directed.
  - Clarify the reconnaissance mission, company mission and intent, and scheme of maneuver.
  - Allocate time for your own reconnaissance and planning to permit a rendezvous with the platoon commander at the designated time and place.
  - Conduct reconnaissance to determine —

- Extent and location of reported and suspected enemy positions.
- Rocket or machine gun fire required to destroy or neutralize these enemy positions.
- Location of key terrain features in the company zone of action and their probable influence on the company scheme of maneuver.
- Avenues of approach to these key terrain features.
- Avenues of approach for enemy armor.
- Confirmation of the designated section position area.
- Selection of general weapons positions, field of fire, and specific targets for each squad.
- Determination of safety limits for supporting fires.
- Displacement method required to maintain continuous fire support.
- Fire control means for coordination.

- Submit recommendations to the platoon commander at the appointed time and place to include —

  - Method of employment of squads.

  - Location of targets and method of engagement.

  - Location of a position area and field of fire for each squad.

  - Displacements required and methods of displacement.

  - Fire control means.

  - As appropriate, employment of weapons for antimechanized defense.

  - Employment of section weapons in consolidation of objectives and continuation of the attack.

On receipt of the platoon commander's order —

- Take maps, notebook, and pencil, and ensure a complete understanding of the section's mission.

- Begin planning:

  - Allocate time for —

    - Further reconnaissance and planning, as required.
    - Squad leaders' reconnaissance and planning.
    - Section movement forward from the assembly area.

  - Using METT-T, continue an estimate of the situation based on the content of the platoon commander's attack order, the supported unit's scheme of maneuver, and previously conducted reconnaissance.

  - Formulate a tentative plan to implement the section mission.

- Arrange for —

  - Movement of the section forward from the assembly area, to include detachments.

  - A reconnaissance route and schedule to facilitate prearranged meetings with supported rifle unit leaders for coordination.

- Make reconnaissance:

  - Select a vantage point from which to orient squad leaders, and a covered position nearby from which to issue the order.

  - Determine enemy location, strength, and disposition.

  - Select a position for each squad.

  - Determine target assignments for squads and safety limits prescribed.

- Locate covered routes forward to initial squad positions.
- Effect coordination with supported unit leaders, to include positioning of weapons, confirmation of the fire support plan, consolidation, and support of continuation of the attack.
- Determine the effect of signals prescribed for fire control.
- Select covered routes and objectives for displacement, as prescribed.

■ Complete the plan:
- Complete an estimate of the situation, to include continuation of the attack.
- Assign specific position area and targets for each squad based on mission of the supported unit (scheme of maneuver), observation, sector of fire, and effective range of weapons.
- Establish fire control measures, as prescribed, for each squad, to include time or signal for opening, shifting, and ceasing fires, rate of fire, and safety limits.
- Prescribe displacement instructions to include —
    - Time or signal for displacement.
    - Method (unit or echelon).
    - Displacement route.
    - Displacement objective.
    - Mission at the displacement objective.
- Provide for security at all gun positions and during all unit movements. Ensure continuous use of camouflage.
- Ensure that all pertinent extracts from the platoon commander's order are considered in completing the plan.

- Determine the location of your own position from which to best control fires of the section.
- Issue the order:
  - Orient subordinates, and ensure a thorough understanding of the orientation.
  - Utilize the standard five paragraph order (see appendix A).
  - Ensure a thorough understanding of the order.
- Supervise —
  - Squad leaders' planning.
  - Effecting detachments.
  - Positioning of squads.
  - Preparation of squad positions.
- Conduct the attack:
  - Commence fire support at the prescribed time, or on order.
  - Maintain fire control and coordination.
  - Continue the estimate of the situation throughout the attack and recommend changes to employment of section weapons, as appropriate.
  - Supervise displacement of the section to ensure continuous fire support and accomplishment of follow-on missions.
  - Maintain unit security during displacements.
  - Coordinate with rifle unit leaders, as directed, to ensure the protection of crew-served weapons and support on the objective.

- Expedite casualty and ammunition status reports from squad leaders.
- Reorganize promptly to reestablish subordinate chains of command and replace key billets made vacant by casualties.
- Redistribute ammunition and replenish, if required.
- Evacuate casualties.
- Establish unit security at all gun positions.
- Report the situation to the platoon commander to include —
  - Enemy situation.
  - Friendly casualties and ammunition status.
  - Information concerning prisoners of war, captured documents, and captured material.
  - Recommendations concerning nonorganic fire support to augment section fires.

- In accordance with the assigned mission, either prepare to support the continuation of the attack, as directed, or supervise the continued organization of the ground for defense, as directed.

NIGHT ATTACK

In the nonilluminated night attack, the following special considerations are integrated with the procedures prescribed for the daylight attack on page 5-9. The weapons platoon section leader will —

- Plan and conduct reconnaissance to —
  - Locate routes to the objective.
  - Locate suitable support-by-fire positions.
  - Locate prominent terrain features to guide displacement to the objective.
  - Determine azimuths.
  - Locate obstacles and determine the means to overcome them.
- Prescribe control measures as necessary and in consonance with those prescribed by the platoon commander. Consider the following in order to facilitate control and coordination:
  - Control points.
  - Flare discipline.
  - Individual conduct.
  - Movement forward from the PLD and support-by-fire positions on order.

- Commencement of assault and supporting fires.
- Primary and alternate signal means to control movement and fire support.

- Plan a rehearsal of the section for a night attack.
- Prepare for the attack:
  - Lay weapons on targets during daylight, when possible.
  - Brief the entire section on details of the operation.
  - Ensure attached squads receive the order from the rifle platoon commander.
  - Be familiar with the missions assigned to attached squads.
  - Conduct a rehearsal with particular emphasis on flare discipline, radio discipline, and individual conduct, including movement, maintaining distance and intervals, light and noise discipline, and security measures.
  - Supervise troop preparations to include —
    - Individual camouflage.
    - Silencing equipment and clothing.
    - Removing or dulling shiny items.
    - Segregating equipment not required for the attack.
    - Issuing ammunition and pyrotechnics.
    - Checking weapons.
- Conduct the attack:
  - Exercise strict noise, light, and flare discipline.
  - Report section readiness for the assault to the platoon commander.

- Supervise actions on the objective.

OTHER OFFENSIVE OPERATIONS

The following special considerations are integrated with the procedures prescribed for the weapons section in the daylight attack (page 5-9), as appropriate for each type of operation.

Section in the Tank-Infantry Attack

The weapons platoon section leader will —

- Determine likely locations of enemy antitank weapons.
- Supervise a briefing of the section on safety precautions.
- Supervise a rehearsal with the tank unit.

Section in the Mechanized Infantry Attack

The weapons platoon section leader will —

- Supervise a rehearsal with supporting vehicles, to include mounting and dismounting procedures, actions on dismounting, and communication procedures.

Section in the Attack of Fortified Areas

The weapons platoon section leader will —

- Conduct a detailed reconnaissance to determine the location and extent of —
  - Individual emplacements to include —
    - Type of construction.
    - Number of embrasures.
    - Types of weapons and their fields of fire.
    - Entrances, exits, and air vents.
    - Location and extent of defending troops providing supporting small arms fire.
  - Supporting fortifications in assigned and adjacent zones.
  - Underground fortifications.
  - Natural and artificial obstacles.
  - Strong and weak points in enemy defense.
- Develop a plan that provides for fires to support obstacle breaching operations and emplacement seizure.

Section in the Attack of Urban Terrain

The weapons platoon section leader will —

- Conduct a reconnaissance in order to —
  - Select streets and alleys that provide the best killing zones to support the attack.

- Coordinate with supported units concerning signals for lifting, shifting, or ceasing of fires within killing zones.

River-Crossing Operations

The weapons platoon section leader will —

■ Conduct a rehearsal with supporting vehicles, if practicable, to include loading and unloading procedures, actions on unloading, and communication procedures.

Defensive Combat

In addition to the general duties prescribed on page 5-1, the weapons platoon section leader is responsible for performing the following actions during defensive combat.

SECTION IN THE DEFENSE

On receipt of the platoon defense order, the weapons platoon section leader will —

■ Take map, notebook, and pencil, and ensure a complete understanding of the section mission and fire control measures.

■ Begin planning:
- Allocate available time for —
    - Personal reconnaissance and planning.
    - Squad leader reconnaissance and planning.

- Movement of the section forward from the assembly area.
- Organization of section defensive areas.

■ Using METT-T, make an estimate of the situation based on the platoon defense plan and reconnaissance.

■ Arrange for —

- Attachment of units, as directed.
- Movement of the section forward from the assembly area.
- A reconnaissance route and schedule to facilitate prearranged meetings with rifle platoon commanders for coordination, as required.
- Participation of squad leaders in the reconnaissance, as required.
- A time and tentative place to issue the order.

■ Make further reconnaissance, as necessary, to include —

- Selecting a vantage point from which to orient subordinate unit leaders and issue the order. (Notify squad leaders of time and place to receive order.)
- Confirming positions, principal directions of fire (PDFs), final protective lines (FPLs), and sectors of fire.
- Completing an analysis of the terrain within and adjacent to the assigned company defense and security areas with emphasis on OCOKA.
- Effecting coordination with supported unit commanders in accordance with the prearranged schedule. In effecting the coordination, consider the employment of weapons in general

support of the defense and close-in protection for crew-served weapons.

- Complete the plan:

  - Complete an estimate of the situation.

  - Assign position location, FPL/PDF, as well as a sector of fire considering —

    - Mission of the section.
    - Observation and fields of fire.
    - Effective range of weapons.

  - Prescribe fire control measures for each squad to include —

    - Time or signal for opening fire, shifting fire, ceasing fire, and firing the final protective fire (FPF).
    - Rate of fire.
    - Safety limits.

  - Provide for security at all gun positions.

  - Ensure proper use of camouflage.

  - Ensure that all pertinent extracts from the platoon commander's order are considered in completing the plan.

  - Determine your own position from which the control of fires can best be effected.

- Issue the order:

  - Orient subordinate unit leaders, and ensure a thorough understanding of the orientation.

  - Utilize the standard order form (see appendix A).

- Ensure a thorough understanding of the commander's intent and concept of operations.

■ Supervise —
  - Subordinate unit planning.
  - Preparation and organization of the ground, with emphasis on security, emplacement construction, and camouflage.

■ Submit a fire plan sketch to include —
  - Positions.
  - Sector of fire for each squad.
  - FPL/PDF for each machine gun team and/or squad.
  - Planned targets and FPF for each mortar squad.

■ Conduct the defense:
  - Notify the platoon commander of enemy activity.
  - Maintain fire discipline and control.
  - On order or signal, fire final protective fires.
  - Inform the platoon commander of the situation at all times, making recommendations for changes in employment, as directed.
  - When the enemy is repelled —
    ▪ Cease final protective fires, as directed.
    ▪ Maintain pursuit by fire until targets cease to exist.
    ▪ Reorganize.
    ▪ Evacuate casualties.
    ▪ Redistribute and resupply ammunition.

SECTION IN THE DEFENSE OF URBAN TERRAIN

In the defense in urban terrain, the following special considerations are integrated with the procedures prescribed for the section in the defense on page 5-19. The weapons platoon section leader will —

- Conduct reconnaissance:
  - Locate building(s) to be occupied and prescribed primary, alternate, and supplementary positions.
- Direct the preparation of building(s) to be occupied:
  - Barricade windows, doors, and other openings.
  - Remove drain pipes, vines, or projections which may assist the enemy in gaining outside access to the upper floors or roofs.
  - Sandbag positions in upper floors for protection against fires from below.
  - Construct barricades in rooms for protection from grenades.
- Report the location of booby traps to the platoon commander.

Relief Operations

In addition to the general duties prescribed on page 5-1, the weapons platoon section leader is responsible for the following actions during relief operations.

RELIEF IN PLACE

Responsibilities of the Incoming Section Leader

- Attach squads, as directed, to the incoming rifle platoons in whose areas their positions are planned.
- Conduct a daylight reconnaissance to include —
  - Inspection of crew-served weapons to be exchanged in the position for completeness and serviceability, if applicable.
  - Position, sector of fire, and final protective line (FPL)/principal directions of fire (PDF) for each machine gun squad.
  - Positions for rockets or mortars, as applicable.
  - Dead space in machine gun final protective fires (FPFs).
  - Alternate and supplementary positions for machine guns or shoulder-launched multipurpose assault weapons (SMAWs), as applicable.
  - Routes of resupply.
- Make recommendations regarding exchange of machine guns or mortars to the weapons platoon commander, if applicable.
- Supervise the exchange of machine guns or mortars, if applicable.
- Upon completion of relief, receive control of the weapons from rifle platoons and employ them in accordance with the assigned mission.

Responsibilities of the Outgoing Section Leader

- Attach squads to rifle platoons, as directed.
- Assist the incoming section leader in his reconnaissance.
- Supervise the exchange of any crew-served weapon, as applicable.
- Resume control of squads in company assembly area unless otherwise directed.

PASSAGE OF LINES

In the passage of lines, the following special considerations are integrated into the procedures prescribed for the daylight attack (page 5-9) or night attack (page 5-15), as appropriate.

Responsibilities of the Attacking Unit Section Leader

- Conduct a daylight reconnaissance with emphasis on —
  - Assembly area.
  - Route(s) to the line of departure (LD) or firing positions.
  - Area(s) of passage.
  - Gaps or lanes in minefields and wire obstacles.
  - Disposition of the weapons of the unit in contact.
- Make recommendations to the platoon commander for integrating the fires of the unit in contact section into the fire support plan for the attack.

Responsibilities of the Unit in Contact Section Leader

- Assist the attacking unit section leader on his reconnaissance.
- Provide fire support, as directed.

Retrograde Operations

In addition to the general duties prescribed on page 5-1, the weapons platoon section leader is responsible for the following actions during retrograde operations.

WITHDRAWAL AND DELAYING ACTION

The weapons platoon section leader will —

- Issue a warning order to provide for maximum use of daylight for preparation and reconnaissance, subordinate planning, and reasons for movement.
- Attach weapons squads, as directed, to platoons in whose areas they are located for movement to the rear.
- When moving to a new defensive position, carry out the troop leading procedures prescribed for the section in the defense (page 5-19).
- Resume control of the section in the company assembly area.

CHAPTER 6

WEAPONS PLATOON
Squad Leader

The **mission** of the **machine gun squad** is to provide supporting machine gun fires for maneuvering or defending elements of the rifle company.

The **mission** of the **assault squad** is to provide close-in antitank protection and assault fires against fortified areas and obstacles. It further provides a limited demolitions capability for destruction and reduction of fortified positions and obstacles.

The **mission** of the **mortar squad** is to provide close and continuous fire in support of the rifle company scheme of maneuver or defensive fire plan.

This chapter discusses the duties of the **weapons platoon squad leader.**

General Duties

In addition to the procedures prescribed for all troop leaders in appendix A, the weapons platoon squad leader will —

- Conduct technical and tactical training of the squad, as directed.

- Control the squad and lead it in all tactical movements.

- Select the exact firing position for each team within the position assigned by the section leader.

- Supervise the preparation and occupation of firing positions, to include continuous camouflage.

- Designate a sector of fire and targets for each machine gun.

- Observe and control the squad fires. Replenish ammunition, as required.

- Supervise first echelon maintenance of weapons and equipment through frequent inspection.

Amphibious Operations

In addition to the general duties prescribed on page 6-1, the weapons platoon squad leader is responsible for the following actions during amphibious operations.

PRE-EMBARKATION DUTIES

The weapons platoon squad leader will —

- Ensure the squad attends all platoon/section instruction.
- Conduct training of the squad, as directed.
- Prepare the squad for pre-embarkation inspections.

- Supervise the squad in making/tagging of weapons, equipment, and baggage for embarkation.
- Assemble the squad in proper uniform at the designated time for embarkation.

DUTIES ABOARD SHIP

The weapons platoon squad leader will —

- Assign individual bunks and supervise the stowage of gear.
- Ensure the squad attends all briefings and periods of instruction.
- Supervise the policing of the squad berthing area, and report discrepancies in ship's facilities to the section leader.
- Enforce applicable ship's regulations.
- Ensure care, cleaning, and security of weapons.
- Prepare the squad for all equipment and personnel inspections.
- Instruct the men on their specific duties afloat and ashore.
- Conduct training of the squad, as directed.

DUTIES DURING SHIP-TO-SHORE MOVEMENT

The weapons platoon squad leader will —

- Assemble the squad in the assembly area.

- Inspect the squad prior to debarkation for the proper rigging of equipment and lashing of crew-served weapons in the assembly area.

- On calling away of the boat team, lead the squad to the debarkation station.

- Inspect the squad for the proper rigging of individual weapons at the debarkation station.

- Supervise the positioning of the squad in landing craft, amphibious vehicle, or rigid raiding craft (RRC)/combat rubber raiding craft (CRRC).

DUTIES DURING ASSAULT

The weapons platoon squad leader will —

- Regain control of separated teams as soon as possible and reorganize, as required.

- Gain contact with the section leader or supported platoon commander after debarkation.

- Deliver fire immediately on suitable targets to assist troops in clearing the beach area.

- Search for appropriate targets and control fires in support of the attack as planned or as directed.

- Report the situation promptly to the section leader or supported rifle platoon commander, to include regaining control, casualties, ammunition status, and change of positions.

Helicopterborne Operations

In addition to the general duties prescribed on page 6-1, the weapons platoon squad leader is responsible for the following actions during helicopterborne operations.

TRAINING DUTIES

The weapons platoon squad leader will —

- Conduct squad training, as directed, in —
  - Embarkation and debarkation procedures, including stowage of machine guns, mortars, shoulder-launched multipurpose assault weapons (SMAWS), and ammunition.
  - Conduct in flight.
  - Preparation and use of manifest tags.
  - Safety precautions.
  - Emergency procedures.
  - Use of emergency equipment.
- Know the duties of the heliteam leader, as described in appendix C.
- Ensure a thorough understanding of —
  - Heliteam organization.
  - Actions in the assembly area, holding area, pickup zone, loading point, and the landing site/zone.

- Initial ground orientation in the objective area by use of compass and terrain features.

DUTIES IN THE ASSEMBLY AREA

The weapons platoon squad leader will —

- Assemble the squad and ensure that it is properly equipped.
- Supervise the preparation of manifest tags.
- Carry out the duties of heliteam leader/assistant leader, if applicable.

DUTIES DURING INITIAL GROUND ACTION

The weapons platoon squad leader will —

- Deliver fire immediately on suitable targets to assist the supported unit in clearing the landing site.
- Regain control of separated teams as soon as possible and reorganize, as required.
- Search for appropriate targets and control fires in support of the attack as planned or as directed.
- Report the situation promptly to the section leader or supported rifle platoon commander, to include regaining control, casualties, ammunition status, and change of positions.

Offensive Combat

In addition to the general duties prescribed on page 6-1, the weapons platoon squad leader will perform the following actions during offensive combat.

MOVEMENT TO CONTACT — FOOT MARCH

- Assign a sector of observation to each team.
- Maintain march discipline.
- During halts assign air sentinels, guns, and team sectors of fire.

MOVEMENT TO CONTACT — MOTORIZED MARCH

In addition to the duties described above for a foot march, the following considerations apply to security missions assigned on a motorized march. The weapons platoon squad leader will —

- Utilize observation and reconnaissance by fire.
- Provide flank security by observation and reconnaissance by fire.
- Provide active air defense by assigning air sentinels and engaging all attacking aircraft.

DUTIES IN THE ASSEMBLY AREA

The weapons platoon squad leader will —

- Assign team areas.
- Provide security, as directed.
- Supervise actions taken to prepare or improve cover.
- Exercise continuous camouflage discipline to include —
  - Removal of excess soil from position.
  - Proper use and timely replacement of natural camouflage material.
  - Disposal of trash.
  - Control of individual movement to avoid creating visible paths.
- Supervise the care and cleaning of weapons and equipment.
- Enforce light and noise discipline.
- Enforce field sanitation measures.
- Ensure segregation of equipment, as directed.
- Inspect each individual for proper ammunition, rations, water, and special equipment, as directed.
- Report at the designated time and place to receive the section leader's order.
- Conduct applicable troop leading steps (see appendix A).
- Supervise the squad in specialized training and/or rehearsals.

DAYLIGHT ATTACK

On receipt of the section leaders' order, the weapons platoon squad leader will—

- Take notebook and pencil and ensure a complete understanding of the squad's mission with emphasis on the supported unit scheme of maneuver, target assignments, and fire control measures.
- Begin planning:
  - Allocate time for reconnaissance and movement of the squad forward from the assembly area.
  - Using METT-T, make an estimate of the situation based on the section leaders' order and supported unit's scheme of maneuver.
  - Formulate a tentative plan to implement the squad mission.
- Arrange for —
  - Movement forward from the assembly area or detachment of squad.
  - A reconnaissance route and schedule to facilitate coordination with the supported rifle unit leader.
- Make reconnaissance:
  - Select a vantage point from which to orient team leaders, and a covered position nearby from which to issue the order.
  - Determine enemy location, strength, and disposition.
  - Locate key terrain features considered in the company scheme of maneuver.

- Locate the avenues of approach used to these key terrain features.
- Locate likely avenues of approach for the enemy armor or mechanized force.
- Select specific weapons positions and specific targets for teams.
- Determine safety limits for squad fires.
- Effect coordination with the supported unit leader, to include positioning of weapons, confirmation of the fire support plan, and continuation of the attack.
- Determine the effect of signals prescribed for fire control.
- Select covered routes and displacement positions, as prescribed.

- Complete the plan:
  - Complete an estimate of the situation, to include METT-T and continuation of the attack.
  - Assign a specific position area and targets for each team based on the mission of the supported unit (scheme of maneuver), observation and sector of fire, and effective range of weapons.
  - Establish fire control measures, as prescribed, to include —
    - Times to coordinate and signal for opening fire, shifting fire, amd ceasing fire.
    - Rate of fire.
    - Safety limits.

- Prescribe the method of displacement of the squad considering —
    - Mission at the displacement objective.
    - Displacement objective.
    - Route of displacement.
    - Time or signal for displacement.
- Provide for security at the squad position and during all squad movement.
- Ensure continuous camouflage of materiel and personnel.
- Ensure all pertinent extracts from the section leaders' order are considered in completing plan.
- Determine your own position from which to best control the fires of the squad.

■ Issue the order:
- Orient subordinates, and ensure a thorough understanding of the orientation.
- Utilize the standard order form (see appendix A).
- Ensure a thorough understanding of the order.

■ Supervise the team leaders' planning, positioning of teams, and preparation of the team

■

■ 's positions.

■ Conduct the attack:
- Commence fire support at the prescribed time, or on order.
- Maintain fire control and coordination.

- Continue the estimate of the situation throughout the attack, and recommend changes to employment of the squad, as appropriate.

- Displace the squad to ensure continuous close fire support and prompt positioning of teams to cover consolidation of the seizure of objective, when directed.

- Maintain unit security during displacements.

- Coordinate with the rifle unit leader, as directed, to ensure protection of crew-served weapons and support of actions on the objective.

- Expedite casualty and ammunition status reports from team leaders.

- Reorganize promptly to reestablish subordinate chains of command and replace key billets made vacant by casualties.

- Reorganize and replenish the ammunition promptly, if required.

- Evacuate casualties.

- Establish unit security at gun positions.

- Report the situation to the section leader to include —
  - Enemy situation.
  - Friendly casualties.
  - Information concerning prisoners of war, captured documents, and captured material.
  - Recommendation concerning nonorganic fire support to augment squad fires.

- In accordance with the assigned mission, either be prepared to support the continuation of the attack, as directed, or supervise the continued organization of the ground for defense, as directed.

NIGHT ATTACK

In the nonilluminated night attack, the following special considerations are integrated with the procedures prescribed for the daylight attack on page 6-9. The weapons platoon squad leader will —

- Conduct a reconnaissance, as directed:
  - Locate terrain features and routes covered in the order.
  - Locate support-by-fire positions.
  - Determine azimuths.
- Ensure a thorough understanding of —
  - Control points.
  - Individual flare, light, and noise discipline.
  - Prescribed signals.
  - Actions upon discovery.
- Plan for rehearsals, as directed.
- Prepare for the attack:
  - Lay weapons on target(s) during daylight.
  - Brief the squad.
  - Conduct a rehearsal with particular emphasis on —

- Flare discipline.
- Individual conduct, including movement, maintaining distance and intervals, light and noise discipline, and security measures.

• Supervise troop preparations to include —

- Individual camouflage.
- Silencing equipment and clothing.
- Removing or dulling shiny items.
- Segregating equipment not required.
- Issuing ammunition and pyrotechnics.
- Checking weapons.

■ Conduct the attack:

• Exercise strict noise, light, and flare discipline.

• Report readiness of the squad for the assault to the section leader or rifle platoon commander to whom attached.

• Supervise actions on the objective.

OTHER OFFENSIVE OPERATIONS

The following special considerations are integrated with the procedures prescribed for the daylight attack on page 6-9. The weapons platoon squad leader will perform the following actions as appropriate for each type of operation.

Squad in the Mechanized Infantry Attack

Weapons squads generally support the rifle platoon during movement and are mounted with the rifle squads of the platoon they are supporting. Weapons squads may revert to general support of the company during a dismounted attack (assault squads normally remain attached to the rifle platoon). The following requires special consideration by the weapons platoon squad leader:

- Be familiar with section leader's duties for the section in the tank-infantry attack (page 5-17).

- Supervise a rehearsal with supporting vehicles, to include mounting and dismounting procedure, actions on dismounting, and communication procedures (to include visual signals).

- When attacking dismounted with tanks, brief the squad on safety precautions and rehearse mounting and dismounting procedures.

Squad in the Attack of Fortified Areas

The weapons platoon squad leader will —

- Conduct a detailed reconnaissance to determine the location and extent of —

  - Individual emplacements to include —
    - Type of construction.
    - Number of embrasures.
    - Types of weapons and their fields of fire.
    - Entrances, exits, and air vents.
    - Location and number of defending troops providing supporting small arms fire.

  - Supporting fortifications in assigned and adjacent zones.

- Underground fortifications.
- Natural and artificial obstacles.
- Strong and weak points in enemy defense.
- Positions for platoon elements.
- Approaches to fortified areas.

■ Develop a plan that provides for fires to support obstacle breaching operations and emplacement seizure.

Squad Attacking in Urban Terrain

The weapons platoon squad leader will —

■ Conduct reconnaissance to —

- Select streets and alleys that provide the best killing zones to support the attack.
- Coordinate with supported units concerning signal for lifting, shifting, or ceasing of fires within killing zones.

River-Crossing Operations

The weapons platoon squad leader will —

■ Conduct a rehearsal with supporting vehicles, if practicable, to include loading and unloading procedures, actions on unloading, and communication procedures.

Defensive Combat

In addition to the general duties prescribed on page 6-1, the weapons platooon section leader is responsible for the following actions during defensive combat.

SQUAD IN THE DEFENSE

On receipt of the section leader's order, the weapons platoon squad leader will —

- Take notebook and pencil, and ensure a complete understanding of both the squad mission and fire control measures.

- Allocate available time for personal reconnaissance and planning, movement of squad forward from the assembly area, and organization of the squad.

- Using METT-T, make an estimate of situation based on the defense order, commander's intent, and reconnaissance.

- Arrange for —

  - Attachment of the squad, if directed.

  - Movement of squad forward from the assembly area.

  - A reconnaissance route and schedule to facilitate the prearranged meeting with the rifle unit leader for coordination, as required.

  - A time and tentative place to issue the order.

- Make reconnaissance, as necessary, to include —

- Selecting a vantage point from which to orient team leaders and issue the order. (Notify them of time and place to receive order.)
- Locating positions, final protective lines (FPLs), principal directions of fire (PDFs), and sectors of fire and/or responsibility.
- Completing an analysis of terrain within and adjacent to the assigned defense and security areas, emphasizing OCOKA.
- Effecting coordination with the supported unit leader in the area where the squad is to be located. This concerns the general support of the defense and close-in protection for crew-served weapons.

■ Complete the plan:
- Using METT-T, complete an estimate of the situation.
- Assign a position, FPL, PDF, and sector of fire/responsibility for each team, as directed.
- Prescribe positive control measures for the squad to include —
    - Signal/time for opening fire, shifting fire, ceasing fire, and firing the final protective fire (FPF).
    - Rate of fire.
    - Safety limits.
- Establish security at gun positions and ensure maximum use of camouflage.
- Ensure all pertinent extracts from the section leader's order are considered in completing the plan.

- Determine your own position from which the control of fires can best be effected.

■ Issue the order:

- Orient subordinates, and ensure a thorough understanding of the orientation.
- Utilize the standard order form (see appendix A).
- Ensure a thorough understanding of the order.

■ Supervise —

- Subordinate planning.
- Preparation and organization of the ground with emphasis on security, emplacement construction, and camouflage.
- Preparation of range cards.

■ Submit a fire plan sketch, to include positions, sector of fire/responsibility for each team, FPL/PDF for each machine gun, and targets and FPF for each mortar.

■ Conduct the defense:

- Notify the section leader/rifle platoon commander of enemy activity.
- Maintain fire discipline and control.
- On order or signal, fire final protective fires.
- Inform the section leader of the situation at all times.
- When the enemy is repelled —
  ■ Cease final protective fires, as directed.
  ■ Maintain pursuit by fire until targets cease to exist.

- Reorganize.
- Redistribute and resupply ammunition.
- Evacuate casualties.

SQUAD IN THE DEFENSE OF URBAN TERRAIN

In the defense of urban terrain, the following special considerations are integrated with the procedures prescribed for the squad in the defense on page 6-17. The weapons platoon squad leader will —

- Conduct a reconnaissance of assigned primary, alternate, and supplementary position(s), and prepare the building(s) to be occupied:
  - Screen or block windows, doors, and other openings.
  - Remove drain pipes, vines, and projections which may assist enemy in gaining outside access to upper floors or roofs.
  - Sandbag positions in upper floors for protection from fires from below.
  - Construct barricades in rooms for protection from grenades.
  - Prepare interior of selected buildings for safe firing of the shoulder-launched multipurpose assault weapon (SMAW), if required.
- Report the location of booby traps to the section leader.

Relief Operations

In addition to the general duties prescribed on page 6-1, the weapons platoon squad leader will perform the following actions during relief operations.

RELIEF IN PLACE

Responsibilities of the Incoming Squad Leader

- Report to the section leader or rifle platoon commander to whom you are attached for movement.
- Conduct a daylight reconnaissance to include —
  - Location of squad release point and route to position.
  - Position, sector of fire, and final protective line (FPL)/principal direction of fire (PDF) for each machine gun.
  - Positions for assault teams or mortars, as applicable.
  - Alternate and supplementary positions and missions for machine guns, assault teams, or mortars, as applicable.
  - Routes for resupply.
- When involved in the exchange of crew-served weapons, inspect weapons for completeness and serviceability and check range cards.
- Conduct a thorough briefing of team leaders.
- Execute relief on order.
- Allow time for team leaders to be oriented by the team leader they are relieving.

- Upon completion of relief, and on order, carry out the defensive mission assigned.

Responsibilities of the Outgoing Squad Leader

- Report to the rifle platoon commander to whom you are attached for movement.
- Assist the incoming squad leader on his reconnaissance.
- Brief the incoming squad leader on the sector of fire, final protective line (FPL)/principal direction of fire (PDF), mutual support, etc.
- Conduct personal reconnaissance of the withdrawal route and the squad assembly area.
- Execute relief of the squad on order.
- Allow time for team leaders to orient the team leader relieving them.
- Upon completion of relief, and on order, move the squad to the squad assembly area.
- Revert to the control of the section leader in the company assembly area.

PASSAGE OF LINES

The squad leader of a unit executing a passage of lines carries out the procedures prescribed for the daylight attack (page 6-9) or the night attack (page 6-13), as appropriate. He further ensures that the passage of lines is effected in accordance with the attack order of the section leader or leader of the unit to which attached.

The squad leader of the unit being passed through will provide fire support, as directed.

Retrograde Operations

In addition to the general duties prescribed on page 6-1, the weapons platoon squad leader is responsible for the following actions during retrograde operations.

WITHDRAWAL

The weapons platoon squad leader will —

- Inform the men of the reason for movement.
- Report to the platoon commander to whom attached for movement to the rear.
  - Make recommendations regarding the team to remain with the detachment left in contact.
  - Attach the team to the rifle squad designated as the detachment left in contact, as directed.
- Conduct a reconnaissance of the squad assembly area and the route to the platoon assembly area.

- Conduct a thorough briefing of the men.

- On order, withdraw the remainder of the squad to the squad assembly area.

- Lead the squad to the platoon assembly area.

- Ensure rapid and quiet movement once withdrawal has commenced.

- Resume control of the team left with the detachment and left in contact in the company assembly area.

DELAYING ACTION

In planning and executing a delaying action, the squad leader utilizes the prescribed procedures for withdrawing the squad found on page 6-23. The following special considerations apply to the organization of the delaying position. The weapons platoon squad leader will —

- Report to the section leader or platoon commander to whom attached.

- Organize the assigned position.

- Provide long-range fire, as directed.

- Increase fire as the enemy approaches position.

- Inform the section leader or platoon commander of the situation.

- Withdraw on order.

(reverse blank)

APPENDIX A

TROOP LEADING PROCEDURES

Troop Leading Steps

- Begin planning:
  - Use METT-T to begin estimates of the situation based on—
    - Content of the order received from the next senior echelon.
    - Terrain orientation as seen from a vantage point, map, or aerial photograph.
  - Plan use of available time for—
    - Personal reconnaissance and planning.
    - Subordinates' reconnaissance and planning.
    - Movement of the unit when movement and planning cannot be conducted concurrently.
  - Formulate a tentative plan of action based on the preliminary estimate of the situation, the higher commander's order, and the commander's intent one and two levels up.
- Arrange for—
  - Reconnaisance.

- Movement of the unit, to include the route, persons to accompany the commander/leader, and the schedule of prearranged meetings with adjacent and supporting unit leaders.
- Issuance of the order. Subordinate leaders are notified of time and place where the order will be issued.
- A time and place for prearranged meetings with adjacent and supporting unit leaders for coordination.

■ Make reconnaissance:
- Revise the estimate of the situation and preliminary plan, as necessary.
- Select a vantage point from which to orient subordinates.
- Effect coordination with adjacent and supporting unit leaders, as planned.
- Confirm tactical control measures.

■ Complete the plan:
- Receive recommendations.
- Complete the estimate and arrive at a decision.
- Prepare the order.

■ Issue the order:
- Orient subordinate leaders.
- Ensure a thorough understanding of the orientation.
    - Utilize standard operation order format.
    - Ensure a thorough understanding of the order.

- Supervise the planning and preparation by subordinates and the conduct of operations.

Estimate of the Situation (METT-T)

The estimate of the situation on the small unit level is made by analysis of the mission (**M**), the enemy (**E**), terrain and weather (**T**), troops and support available (**T**) - time available (**T**). From the estimate the commander/leader determines the best way to accomplish the mission.

MISSION

Make a careful analysis and have a thorough understanding of the assigned tasks and the commander's intent. Examine the mission to determine if additional tasks may be implied in addition to those specified.

ENEMY

Obtain as much of the following information as possible concerning the enemy (**SALUTE**) and his capabilities (**DRAW-D**).

- **SALUTE**
    - Size: Size of the enemy unit(s), to include personnel and combat effectiveness/efficiency, and main effort, if known.
    - Activity: Recent significant actions/movements.
    - Location: Defensive positions, facilities, assembly areas, etc..

- **Unit:** Type of unit and composition.
- **Time:** Currency of sighting or information.
- **Equipment:** Types of weapons and equipment.

■ **DRAW-D**
- **Defend:** Capability to defend. Includes when the defense can be established (hasty and deliberate) and with what size force and type weapon systems.
- **Reinforce:** Capability to reinforce. Includes the capability to reinforce enemy units in contact, not in contact, in the defense, and in the attack. State size of reinforcing unit(s) and the time required to reinforce.
- **Attack:** Capability to attack. Includes the size/strength of the enemy force, time the attack can be conducted, and locations where the enemy can attack with that size force in that time.
- **Withdraw:** Capability to withdraw. Includes the size/strength of the enemy force, speed of the withdrawal, time required to execute the withdrawal, and locations where he is capable of conducting the withdrawal.
- **Delay:** Capability to delay. Includes the size/strength of the delaying force, methods of delay, time required to conduct the delay, length of time the delay can be conducted, and the routes he can delay.

TERRAIN AND WEATHER

■ Consider the following military aspects of terrain from both friendly and enemy viewpoints:

- Observation and fields of fire.

- Cover and concealment, including observation from the air.

- Obstacles, both natural and artificial.

- Key terrain, including features in the adjacent zone or area which may affect the unit's operation.

- Avenues of approach, to include visibility, movement, fire support, and battlefield mobility.

- Higher unit mission, limitations, constraints, area of operations, and boundaries.

- Weather, to include the effects on observation, mobility, individual stamina, and logistics requirements.

- Maneuver space available to both your own and subordinate units. Attempt to provide subordinate units more than one route or choice of form of maneuver.

TROOPS AND SUPPORT AVAILABLE

■ Unit strength and location with respect to the enemy.

■ Logistics capability and requirements.

■ Fire support from higher and adjacent units.

■ Space systems and support available for navigation, communication, target acquisition, and other intelligence collection.

TIME AVAILABLE

- Time available for planning and preparation. The commander/leader should provide two-thirds of the available time to his subordinate for his planning and preparation

- Time necessary to move and/or conduct the operations of your own unit, as well as supporting and adjacent unit(s).

Combat Orders

OPERATION ORDER

This order is prepared and issued in a clear and concise manner and is preceded by a thorough orientation of the area of operations. The orientation should be conducted with the aid of a terrain model from a secure vantage point. At a minimum, the orientation will be aided by a map or sketch of the area.

1. Situation:

    a. Enemy Forces. **SALUTE, DRAW-D,** and most likely/dangerous enemy courses of action. Enemy information is confined to that which may be likely to affect the accomplishment of the mission.
    b. Friendly Forces. HAS-S (Higher, adjacent, supporting, and security). Includes mission, intent, and locations of the next two higher commands, as well as adjacent, and supporting units which may affect the actions of the unit.

c. Attachments and Detachments. Units attached to or detached from your unit for the operation, including the effective time. Existing attachments will be restated.

2. Mission: A clear concise statement of the mission to be accomplished by the unit. Includes essential tasks (specified and implied tasks deemed critical to mission success), and the purpose of the mission (who, what, when, where, and why).

3. Execution:

   a. Commander's Intent. The commander's intent is a clear, concise statement that defines success for the force as a whole by establishing, in advance of events, the desired end state. It contains: the purpose of the operation; the critical vulnerabilities and center of gravity for both enemy and friendly forces; a vision of how the operation will be conducted in a broad scope; a description of the end state with respect to the relationship of the force, the enemy, and the terrain; and a description of how the end state will facilitate future operations.

b. **Concept of Operations.** The concept of operations provides general direction for all subordinate unit operations and extends the commander's intent throughout the entire force. Each subordinate leader develops his own concept of operations in consonance with the higher concept. The concept of operations becomes the basis for task organization, the scheme of maneuver, tasks to subordinates, and identification of critical operations. It should include the initial formations of the unit, distribution of forces, fire support, and actions of the unit as a whole during critical events through completion of the mission.

c. **Tasks.** This subparagraph assigns missions to each committed organic unit in numerical or alphabetical sequence followed by the attached unit(s). It also identifies the subordinate unit(s) designated the main effort.

d. **Reserve.** The next to last subparagraph designates and assigns a mission to the reserve unit.

e. **Coordinating Instructions.** The last subparagraph lists the coordinating instructions common to two or more subordinate units.

4. **Administration and Logistics:** This paragraph contains information or instructions pertaining to rations, ammunition, enemy prisoner of war (EPW) handling and evacuation, aid station, resupply, and administrative matters. Only necessary information is included.

5. Command and Signal:

   a. Communications/signal instructions and information.

   b. Location of the unit commander/leader and the next higher unit commander/leader.

WARNING ORDER

The warning order is issued to alert subordinates to the coming operations. The content follows the same sequence as the operation order. It contains sufficient information and necessary instructions to permit timely preparation and planning for the operation.

COMBAT ORDER (FRAGMENTARY FORM)

The combat order in fragmentary form is issued when time or the situation preclude the issuance of a complete operation order. The content follows the same sequence as the complete order. It contains the mission and essential information to permit the subordinate unit(s) to accomplish the assigned task(s). It must contain the mission and execution.

APPENDIX B

DUTIES OF THE BOAT TEAM AND ASSISTANT BOAT TEAM COMMANDERS

Boat Team Commander

- Organize the boat team by appointing members to key billets.
  - Landing craft —
    - Assign an assistant boat team commander.
  - Assault amphibious vehicle (AAV) —
    - Assign an assistant boat team commander.
  - Rigid raiding craft (RRC)/combat rubber raiding craft (CRRC) —
    - Assign a navigator/assistant navigator, as appropriate, and boat positions 1-8.
- Assign personnel and equipment to positions in the craft/vehicle in accordance with the tactical plan ashore.
- Reconnoiter the route from the troop assembly area to the debarkation station or AAV/RRC/CRRC.
- Muster the boat team in the assembly area at the required times.
- Inspect each member for proper uniform, rations, and ammunition, as well as adjustment of required equipment.

Duties of the Boat Team Commanders   B-2

- Supervise the lashing of crew-served weapons and equipment into the landing craft.

- On order, lead the boat team from the assembly area to the debarkation station/vehicle.

- Form the boat team for debarkation at the debarkation station (not applicable to AAV/RRC/CRRC).

- Report boat team readiness to the debarkation station officer (not applicable to AAV/RRC/CRRC).

- On order, commence and supervise the debarkation.

- Inform the coxswain or crew chief when all men and equipment are aboard.

- Ensure that the men are in their assigned positions and muzzles are all pointed outboard.

- Instruct the crew chief to report when the craft crosses the line of departure, as well as when it is approximately 100m from the beach.

- Upon landing, lead the boat team from the landing craft/vehicle to the assembly point on the beach.

Assistant Boat Team Commander

- Assist the boat team commander in carrying out the duties outlined in the section above.

- Leave the assembly area last and ensure all personnel and equipment assigned to the boat team clear the assembly area.

- Supervise.

APPENDIX C

HELICOPTERBORNE OPERATIONS

Heliteam Leader

- Inspect heliteam members for proper uniform, equipment, and adjustment of equipment in the assembly area.

- Muster heliteam in the assembly area and supervise the preparation of manifest tags.

- Ensure that equipment and supplies assigned to the heliteam are properly located prior to being called to the loading site.

- Collect the manifest tags from heliteam members immediately prior to being called to the loading site.

- Lead heliteam from the assembly area to the holding area and loading point.

- Turn over manifest tags to control personnel at the appropriate time and place.

- Supervise embarkation of the heliteam.

- Assign personnel and equipment to seats or positions in the helicopter.

- Ensure Marines have and wear hearing protection.

- Maintain heliteam discipline.

- Lead heliteam in the debarkation.

Assistant Heliteam Leader

- Assist the heliteam leader, as directed.

- Be familiar with all the duties of the heliteam leader and assume leadership in his absence.

- Check the helicopter to ensure all personnel and equipment have been debarked.

APPENDIX D

INTELLIGENCE PROCEDURES

Reporting Enemy Information

Information on the enemy requires accurate and quick reporting of the WHAT, WHERE, and WHEN. On enemy sighting, the small unit leader dispatches a SALUTE report that includes —

EXAMPLE

S ize	Reinforced squad, approximately 15 enemy.
A ctivity	Moving south in tactical column.
L ocation	Vicinity road junction Rt9 & Rt31, coordinates TD931867.
U nit	Infantry, red patch on left shirt sleeve.
T ime	Sighted at 281545Z Mar93.
E quipment	Small arms, 2 automatic weapons, 1 light machine gun, all are wearing helmets.

Flash-Bang Method of Range Estimation

Sound travels approximately 350 meters per second. When the observer sees the flash or smoke of a weapon or the dust it raises on firing, he starts counting seconds (one thousand-one, one thousand-two, etc.). He stops counting when he hears the sound of the weapon. If he stops on the count of one thousand-three, for example, the range from the observer to the gun is three times 350 meters per second, or 1050 meters. When combined with a good direction using a compass, this technique can help achieve an accurate target location.

Format for Shelling/Mortar/Bomb Reports

The following format is used in either oral or written form for shelling (SHELREP), mortar (MORTREP), or bomb (BOMBREP) reports:

A. Unit or origin (use current call-sign, address group, or code name).

B. Observer's location (a map reference is preferred; however, such a reference must be encoded).

C. Azimuth to enemy gun, grid or magnetic (state which).

D. Time shelling started.

E. Time shelling stopped.

F. Coordinates or description of area shelled.

G. Number, caliber, and type of weapons fired.

H. Nature of fire; i.e., destruction, harassing, registration, etc.

I. Number and type of shells.

J. Flash-bang time in seconds.

K. Damage (usually in code).

- The report must be preceded by the appropriate code word; i.e., SHELREP, MORTREP, or BOMBREP.

- Paragraph headings are NOT transmitted. Only the letter corresponding to the paragraph heading is used.

- Paragraphs which cannot be completed, or are not applicable, will be omitted in the transmission of the report.

- Higher classification may be used when the originator considers prevailing conditions warrant such action.

Handling of Prisoners (Five S's)

- SEARCH   Search prisoners immediately upon capture for weapons and documents or material.

- SEGREGATE   Segregate prisoners into groups: officers, NCOs, privates, deserters, civilians, and females.

- SILENCE   Enforce silence among prisoners at all times.

- SPEED   Evacuation of prisoners to the rear should be effected quickly and humanely.

Intelligence Procedures   D-4

- SAFEGUARD   Provide an escort to safeguard prisoners from abuse and escape.

Instructions to Prisoner-of-War Escorts

- Prevent escape.
- Maintain segregation.
- Enforce silence.
- Prevent anyone from giving prisoners food, drink, or tobacco prior to interrogation.
- No one will talk to prisoners except intelligence personnel.
- Be alert for prisoners destroying or discarding documents or insignia.
- Speed is essential.

Prisoner-of-War and Document/Equipment Tagging

To provide intelligence personnel with needed information, the capturing unit will provide the next higher unit with the date/time of capture, place (or sector) of capture, circumstances of capture, and the unit capturing the prisoner (normally accomplished by completion of a prisoner-of-war tag).

Documents and other material of possible intelligence value are tagged to reflect the above information. When documents and material are removed from prisoners-of-war, the tag will identify the prisoner from whom they were taken.

APPENDIX E

DUTIES OF THE PATROL LEADER

Patrol Organization

Upon receipt of the mission, organize the patrol into elements (general organization). Further organize the elements into teams (special organization) based on planned actions at the objective, anticipated contact, and the known enemy situation. If at all possible, unit integrity should be maintained in organizing the elements and teams.

RECONNAISSANCE PATROL

The patrol leader will —

- Organize the reconnaissance patrol into —
  - Reconnaissance Element: Reconnoiters or maintains surveillance over the objective.
  - Security Element: Secures the objective rallying point, covers likely avenue(s) of approach and provides early warning, and protects the reconnaissance element.
  - Command Element: Composed of the patrol leader and personnel providing support for the entire patrol. For example, a forward observer (FO), a corpsman, and/or a radio operator could be members of the command element.

Duties of the Patrol Leader   E-2

In a small patrol, the patrol leader will also lead the reconnaissance element at the objective.

- When assigned a zone reconnaissance mission, organize patrol into the required number of reconnaissance teams, each responsible for their own security.

COMBAT PATROL

The patrol leader will —

- Organize the combat patrol into—
  - Assault Element: Engages, overcomes, and physically secures the objective.
  - Support Element: Delivers neutralizing and supporting fires.
  - Security Element: In addition to providing security during the movement, the security element should secure the objective rally point (ORP), and isolate the objective area by early warning and blocking avenues of approach to prevent enemy entry or exit from the objective area.
- In a combat patrol, the patrol headquarters is composed of the patrol leader and any personnel not assigned specific tasks within either the assault or security elements.

Patrol Steps

The patrol leader will —

- Study the mission.
- Plan use of available time: (Remaining steps may vary in sequence.)
  - Establish a time schedule for planning and preparation.
  - Use the "reverse planning" technique to ensure time is allocated for all necessary actions.
- Study the friendly and enemy situation:
  - Study dispositions, strengths, and capabilities affecting the mission.
  - Determine how the current friendly and enemy situations will affect the conduct of the patrol. The situation will determine route, size, organization, weapons, and equipment of the patrol.
- Make a map study, to include aerial photographs, sketches, and previous patrol overlays.
  - Study the terrain en route to and return from the objective.
    - Locate terrain features as aids in navigation, likely danger areas, assigned checkpoints, and obstacles.
    - Select tentative rallying points.
    - Determine the influence of the above on organization, formation, and requirements for special equipment.
  - Study the terrain in the vicinity of the objective to determine—

Duties of the Patrol Leader   E-4

- Number of security teams required.
- Route of reconnaissance at objective.
- Support element employment.
- Direction of assault.
- Influence on size and organization.

■ Organize the patrol:

- Determine the elements and teams required to accomplish the mission.
- Organize into general and special organization.

■ Select patrol members:

- Maintain unit integrity.
- Replace men who may jeopardize mission accomplishment.
- Obtain specialists if not assigned.

■ Select weapons and ammunition:

- Determine requirements to accomplish the mission.
- Consider the use of crew-served weapons.

■ Select equipment. Determine the requirements —

- In the objective area.
- Enroute to and return from the objective.
- For control.
- For rations and water.
- For individual equipment.

■ Issue the warning order at the earliest opportunity:

- Issue the order to all patrol members.
- Include the following minimum items of information:
  - A brief statement of enemy and friendly situations.
  - The mission of the patrol exactly as received.
  - General and special organization, and general tasks to the elements and teams.
  - Uniform common to all, including camouflage and identification measures.
  - Weapons, ammunition, and equipment.
  - Who will accompany the patrol leader on reconnaissance, and who will supervise the preparation during the patrol leader's absence.
  - Instructions for obtaining weapons, ammunition, equipment, rations, and water.
  - Chain of command.
  - Time schedule for meals.
  - Time, place, uniform, and equipment for rehearsals and inspections.

- Coordinate —
  - Movement in friendly areas or positions with respect to time and route.
  - Mutual assistance at points of departure and return with the leader of unit or personnel at these points, to include—
    - Guides through wire and minefields.
    - Latest information on enemy.
    - Information on known obstacles.
    - Time of departure and expected time of return.
    - Size of patrol.
    - General route immediately in front of position or area.

Duties of the Patrol Leader   E-6

- Initial rallying point.
- Challenge and password.

- Coordinate on-call targets planned in support of the patrol.

- Supply support with respect to the availability of special equipment.

- Planned route(s) when not designated.

- Communication plan.

  - Radio-wire.
  - Reporting time(s) and situations.
  - Frequencies, alternate frequencies, and call signs.
  - Prearranged code words and/or shackle.
  - Alternate means of communications.
  - Secure voice, cryptographic periods(s), and changeover times(s).
  - Radio silence procedures.

■ Conduct a reconnaissance to include —

- Personal reconnaissance within friendly area(s).

- Visual reconnaissance of terrain over which the patrol will pass.

- Air reconnaissance.

■ Complete detailed plans:

- Assign specific duties for elements, teams, and individuals.

- Complete route and alternate route planning (coordinate).

  - Avoid open areas.

- Avoid obstacles which may be mined, boobytrapped, or covered by fire.
- Avoid ridges that may silhouette the patrol.
- Relate route to assigned checkpoints and tentative rallying points.
- Plan an alternate route far enough removed from the primary route so as to avoid detection by the enemy on the primary route.

• Determine formation(s) and order of movement considering the following:

- Enemy situation and planned action on enemy contact.
- Tactical integrity to enhance control, all-round security, and employment at the objective.
- Control requirements.
- Speed of movement and stealth.
- Terrain and weather effects on control and visibility.
- Dispersion related to control.

• Plan actions at the initial and reentry rally points that provide for mutual recognition, security, and assistance.

• Plan action at rallying points to include —

- Security of rallying points.
- Specified time to wait before continuation.
- Specified portion of the patrol required before continuation.

• Plan action at danger areas to include reconnaissance, security measures, method of crossing, and selection of different recrossing point.

- Plan action upon enemy contact. Organization for movement and planned action must support each other. Plan for chance contact, hasty ambush, immediate assault, counter ambush, and break contact.
- Plan actions at the objective area according to the mission.
  - Reconnaissance Patrols. Consider the following:
    - Patrol leader's reconnaissance.
    - Positioning of the security team(s), as appropriate.
    - Reconnaissance route for the reconnaissance team(s).
    - Sufficient time to accomplish the mission.
    - Dissemination of information to the entire patrol.
    - Withdrawal or rendezvous, as appropriate.
  - Combat Patrols. Consider the following:
    - Positioning security team(s) as appropriate.
    - Patrol leader's reconnaissance with appropriate subordinate leaders.
    - Positioning of assault and support teams, as appropriate. Arrange movement so both assault and support reach positions at approximately the same time.
    - Signals for coordinated action between the assault and support elements.
    - Withdrawal to the objective rallying point.
- Plan for positive control. Consider —
  - Voice and audible sounds.
  - Arm-and-hand signals.
  - Infrared equipment and/or passive night vision equipment.
  - Luminous tape.
  - Formations.

- Accounting for members after enemy contact, during halts, and while crossing danger areas.

• Provide for accurate navigation.

- Assign navigators (compassmen).
- Assign pacers and divide the route into "legs."
- Check and preset compasses prior to departure.

• Provide for positive security on the move and during halts.

• Provide for inspection and rehearsals.

• Provide coordinating instructions to include —

- Arms and ammunition (changes to those prescribed in warning order).
- Uniform and equipment (changes to those prescribed in warning order).
- Handling of wounded and prisoners.
- Signals, to include intrapatrol communications and communications with higher headquarters.
- Challenges and password for use within the patrol and friendly areas.
- Chain of command, to include all members.
- Location of the patrol leader and subordinate leaders.

■ Issue the patrol leader's order:

- Issue order orally and in conjunction with visual aids illustrating planned actions.
- Issue order to all patrol members.

■ Conduct inspections:

- Correct uniform and equipment errors. Check serviceability of special equipment.

- Ensure a thorough understanding of the order by members, to include the general plan of the operation, what each Marine is to do and when to do it, what others are to do as far as their actions concerning that Marine, and challenge, passwords, codes, and signals.

■ Conduct rehearsals:

- Rehearse all planned actions, to include organization for movement and actions —
  - At the objective.
  - At danger areas.
  - In the event of enemy contact.
  - At rally points.
  - On leaving and reentering friendly areas.

- Verify the suitability of equipment.

- Change plans, as required.

- If involved in a night operation, conduct both night and day rehearsals.

■ Supervise and reinspect that all equipment is serviceable (test-fire weapons when feasible) and that nothing is left behind.

APPENDIX F

FIRE SUPPORT REQUESTS

Elements of the Artillery and Mortar Calls for Fire

The call for fire is sent quickly, but clearly enough to be understood, recorded, and read back without error by the fire direction center (FDC) recorder. The normal call for fire is sent in three transmissions consisting of six elements. A description of the three transmissions is provided below.

FIRST TRANSMISSION: OBSERVER IDENTIFICATION WARNING ORDER

This transmission clears the net for the mission and lets the FDC know who is calling for fire and what type of mission is requested. Be prepared to authenticate. The first element of the transmission is the **observer identification** (e.g., "W6F31 this is T5R45"). The second element of the transmission is the **warning order**. The first part of the warning order indicates the type of mission to be fired. One of the following mission types must be stated:

"Adjust Fire": For uncertain or inaccurate target locations where adjustment may be necessary.

"Fire for Effect": For accurate target locations where adjustment is not necessary.

Fire Support Requests F-2

"Immediate Suppression": For quickly delivering a few suppression rounds on a target that is firing on friendly forces.

"Suppression": For quickly delivering a few suppression rounds on a target that may soon take friendly forces under fire.

The second part of the warning order indicates the method to be used in identifying the target location. The grid method (UTM grid coordinates) is standard; nothing is announced here if the grid method will be used. "Polar" is announced here if the polar method will be used (direction and distance from the observer). If the shift method will be used (i.e., target location referenced from known point), announce "shift from" and state the known point used as a reference.

First transmission examples:

"W6F31 this is T5R45, fire for effect, over." (fire for effect, grid method)

"W6F31 this is T5R45, adjust fire, shift from target AF2013, over." (adjust fire, shift method)

"W6F31 this is T5R45, immediate suppression, polar." (immediate suppression, polar method)

SECOND TRANSMISSION: TARGET LOCATION

This transmission contains the **target location** using the method identified in the first transmission. If the grid method is used, announce "grid" followed by the grid coordinates.

  Example: "Grid 123456, over."

If the polar method is used, announce "direction" followed by the direction to the target in mils (or degrees), announce "distance" followed by the distance in meters to the target, and announce "up" or "down" followed by the vertical difference in meters from the observer to the target, if significant.

  Example: "Direction 1200, distance 3000, down 50, over."

If the shift method is used, announce "direction" followed by the direction to the target, announce "left" or "right" followed by the horizontal shift in meters from the known point to the target, and announce "up" or "down" followed by the vertical difference in meters from the known point to the target, if significant.

  Example: "Direction 0800, left 400, over."

Fire Support Requests   F-4

THIRD TRANSMISSION: TARGET DESCRIPTION
METHOD OF ENGAGEMENT
METHOD OF FIRE AND CONTROL

A brief but accurate **target description** is critical in assisting the FDC to select the type and amount of ammunition for the target. Describe what the target is, what the target is doing, the number of elements in the target, the degree of target protection, and the target size and shape, if significant.

The **method of engagement** may be omitted, but the observer must state "danger close" if the target is within 600 meters of friendly forces. The observer may also request a specific type of ammunition, although for the untrained observer it is better left to the FDC to select ammunition based on target description. Shell high explosive (HE) with fuze quick (Q) is standard and need not be stated. Other common shell/fuze combinations that may be requested or provided include —

HE/VT (Variable Time): For troops in the open, in trenches or deep fighting holes, and soft-skinned vehicles.

HE/Delay: For penetration into dense woods, against light earthworks or buildings, or against unarmored vehicles.

WP (White Phosphorus): For vehicles, petroleum, oils, and lubricants (POL) storage areas, ammunition storage areas, and enemy observers.

Smoke: For screening.

DPICM (Dual-Purpose Improved Conventional Munitions): Disperses numerous shape-charged grenades over a large area.

APICM (Anti-Personnel Improved Conventional Munitions): Disperses numerous antipersonnel grenades over a large area.

The **method of fire and control**s normally omitted for untrained observers. However, if the fire is desired at a specific time, the observer may announce "at my command" or "time on target" followed by a specific time for delivery.

Third transmission examples:

"Tank platoon in open, DPICM in effect, time on target 1205, over."

"Infantry company dug in, over."

"Two BTRs in open, at my command, over."

Naval Gunfire Call for Fire

The call for fire is sent to the ship in two transmissions consisting of six elements. A description of the two transmissions is provided below.

**FIRST TRANSMISSION: OBSERVER IDENTIFICATION
WARNING ORDER AND
TARGET NUMBER**

This transmission clears the net for the mission, lets the ship know who is calling for fire, and assigns a target number for the mission. Be prepared to authenticate. The first element of the transmission is the **observer identification** (e.g., "W6F31 this is T5R45"). The second element of the transmission consists of the announcement "fire mission", which serves as **warning order**, and a **target number** assigned from a block of target numbers allocated by the fire support coordination center (FSCC).

Example: "K3Y this is T5R45, fire mission, AB3001, over."

**SECOND TRANSMISSION: TARGET LOCATION
TARGET DESCRIPTION
METHOD OF ENGAGEMENT
METHOD OF CONTROL**

The first element of the second transmission is th**e target location** This element depends on the method of target location. If the grid method is used, announce "grid" followed by the UTM grid coordinates, announce "altitude" followed by the target altitude in meters, and announce "direction" followed by the direction to the target.

    Example: "Grid 123456, altitude 600, direction 1200."

If the polar method is used, announce "direction" followed by the direction to the target in mils (or degrees), announce "distance" followed by the distance in meters to the target, and announce "up" or "down" followed by the vertical difference in meters from the observer to the target, if significant. This method can only be used if the ship knows the observer's location.

    Example: "Direction 1200, distance 3000, down 50."

If the shift method is used, announce "from target number _____" to identify the known point, announce "direction" followed by the direction to the target, announce "left" or "right" followed by the horizontal shift in meters from the known point to the target, and announce "up" or "down" followed by the vertical difference in meters from the known point to the target, if significant. This method can only be used if the ship has recorded the known point's location.

    Example: "From target AF2013, direction 0800, left 400."

A brief but accurate **target description** is important in providing the FSCC with tactical information. Describe what the target is, what the target is doing, the number of elements in the target, the degree of target protection, and the target size and shape, if significant.

Fire Support Requests

Fire Support Requests

The **method of engagement** may be omitted, but the observer must state "danger close" if the target is within 750 meters of friendly forces. The observer may also request a specific type of ammunition if other than the standard shell high explosive (HE) with quick fuze (Q) is desired. Unlike artillery FDCs, ships will not adjust the ammunition fired based on the target description. After selecting ammunition, the observer should identify the number of salvos (or volleys) to be fired. Appropriate ammunition selections include —

HE/CVT (Controlled Variable Time): For troops in the open, in trenches or deep fighting holes, soft-skinned vehicles, and radar installations.

HE/Delay: For penetration into dense woods, against light earthworks or buildings, or against unarmored vehicles.

WP: For vehicles, POL and ammunition storage areas, and enemy observers.

Smoke: For screening.

Spotter adjust (same as artillery adjust fire) is the standard **method of control** and need not be stated. Announce "fire for effect" if target location is accurate and adjustment is not anticipated. "At my command" or "time on target ____" may be announced if the observer desires to control when fires impact.

Second transmission examples:

"Grid 123456, altitude 600, direction 1200, ZSU 23-4 in open, HE/CVT, 5 rounds, fire for effect, over." (fire for effect, grid method, fire when ready)

"Direction 1200, distance 3000, down 50, supply dump, WP, at my command, over." (spotter adjust, polar method, at my command)

"From target number AF2013, direction 0800, left 400, machine gun bunker, HE/Delay, 10 rounds, fire for effect, time on target 1205, over." (fire for effect, shift method, time on target)

Close Air Support

Requests for immediate close air support (CAS) missions are sent to the direct air support center (DASC) but may be processed through a FSCC, if necessary. The format used for immediate requests corresponds to the appropriate line of the joint tactical air request (JTAR). The request is normally sent in one transmission in the following format:

Element	Example
1. Unit Called/ Request Identification	"Budworth this is T5R45 with an immediate CAS request"
2. Mission Category	"Immediate, priority 2"

Fire Support Requests F-10

3. Target Description	"5 armored vehicles moving in column"
4. Target Location	"FD623456"
5. Time on Target	"ASAP"
6. Desired Ordinance/Results	(omit)
7. Final Control	
Call sign	"T5R45"
Frequency	"This net"
Contact point	(omit)
8. Remarks	"Friendly troops, 1000 meters south"

When the aircraft reports in, the close air support terminal controller transmits the brief to the aircrew with essential information for execution of the mission. It is sent in one transmission and follows a nine-line format which is provided below. Reference to line numbers or elements is not required.

Element	**Example**
1. Initial Point (IP) or Attack Position.	"Snake"
2. Heading and Offset	"045, left"
3. Distance	"Twelve point three"

4. Target Elevation   "55"

5. Target Description   "5 armored vehicles moving
                              north to south in column"

6. Target Location   "FD623456"

7. *Type Mark   "WP"

8. *Location of Friendlies   "South 1000"

9. *Egress   "Egress south to ford"

* These elements may be omitted in a limited communcations environment.

APPENDIX G

DUTIES OF LEADERS FOR NBC DEFENSE

Defense Against Nuclear Attack

PRIOR TO THE ATTACK

- Prepare the men tactically and psychologically for nuclear defense.
- Instruct the men on the effects of a nuclear detonation.
- Indoctrinate the men in the protective measures for blast, heat, and nuclear radiation.
- Be alert for the following indications of nuclear attack:
  - Appearance of enemy wearing special equipment and clothing.
  - Unusual enemy movement or withdrawal from forward areas.
  - Registration of heavy artillery with high air bursts.

DURING THE ATTACK

- Do not look at the fire ball.
- Dive for cover instantly.
- Keep head, face, and skin covered.

- Remain under cover until the danger from flying debris has passed.
- Put on a protective mask and gloves.

AFTER THE ATTACK

- Reorganize the unit.
- Report the situation to the senior in the chain of command.
- Reestablish contact with adjacent unit(s).
- Be prepared to continue the mission.
- Take steps to protect the unit from residual radiation, if necessary:
  - Take cover.
  - Use poncho, shelter half, or other material for overhead cover.
  - Keep clothing as dust-free as possible.
  - Report to decontamination station on order.
- Ensure subordinates do not eat or drink anything that has been exposed to contamination.

Defense Against Biological Attack

PRIOR TO THE ATTACK

- Ensure subordinates receive all immunizations and medications.
- Provide the men with serviceable protective masks.
- Instruct the men in the proper wearing and maintenance of masks.
- Maintain physical fitness of the unit through physical conditioning exercises and individual's attention to personal cleanliness and field sanitation.
- Permit the men to eat and drink only approved food and water.
- Instruct the unit on possible indications of attack to include—
  - Aircraft dropping or spraying unidentified substances.
  - New and unusual types of shells or bombs.
  - Smokes of unknown source or nature.
  - An increased occurrence of sick or dead animals.
  - An increase in the number of insects.
  - Weapons not seeming to have any immediate casualty effect.
- Alert higher headquarters and subordinates of a possible attack.

DURING THE ATTACK

- Require the men to wear protective masks.
- Guard against contamination. Have all food and water checked and declared safe before allowing your men to consume it.

Duties of Leaders for NBC Defense

- Require the men to wear their complete field uniform to keep biological agents from reaching the skin. Check to ensure —
  - Shirt and jacket collars are fastened.
  - Sleeves are rolled down and buttoned.
  - Trousers are bloused.
  - Gloves are worn, if available.
- Ensure the men keep their bodies, clothes, and living area clean.
- Report information as to the type or nature of the biological agent to the next higher commander as soon as possible.

AFTER THE ATTACK

- Supervise decontamination measures:
  - Boil water for 15 minutes if not sealed.
  - Boil or wash sealed containers of food thoroughly before the seal is broken.
  - Expose contaminated objects to sunlight.
  - Wash exposed areas with soap and water.
  - Add purification tablets to water.
  - Cook food prior to eating.
- Instruct the men to avoid contaminated areas.
- Observe the men for sickness (may not occur for a few hours to days after contact with the agent).

Defense Against Chemical Attack

PRIOR TO THE ATTACK

- Conduct a thorough training program to indoctrinate your men on the various characteristics of the agents and the three phases of defensive operations; detection, protection, and decontamination.

- Coordinate with NBC personnel for training in the use of special equipment used to identify and detect chemical agents.

- Provide your men with masks and other protective and detection equipment.

- Ensure the men are trained in the use of self-protection, first aid methods, and antidotes.

- Coordinate with NBC personnel for training your men in decontamination procedures.

  - Be alert to detect and sound the alarm for a chemical attack. Indications include—
    - Position under attack by aircraft spray.
    - Smoke or mist of an unknown source is present or approaching.
    - A suspicious odor or liquid is present.
    - You observe one or more of the following symptoms in your men:
      - An unexplained runny nose.
      - A feeling of choking or tightness in the chest or throat.
      - Dimming of vision.
      - Irritation of the eyes.
      - Difficulty in or increased rate of breathing.

DURING THE ATTACK

- Sound the alarm.

- Have the men don masks quickly and take other appropriate protective and first aid measures.

- Move the men upwind and away from smoke and spray, if possible.

AFTER THE ATTACK

- Require the men to wear masks until receiving the command decision to unmask.

- Reorganize and continue the mission.

- Begin first aid and remove casualties.

- Supervise mission-oriented protective posture (MOPP) exchange, if necessary.

- Ensure the men decontaminate weapons, equipment, and living area.

Unmasking Procedures

Unmasking procedures are authorized by a higher authority only.

- Procedures when a detector kit is available:

- A chemical agent detector kit (M256) is used to test for the presence or absence of chemical agents. After determining the absence of chemical agents, two or three individuals unmask for five minutes, then remask and are examined in a shady area for chemical agent symptoms. If no symptoms appear, the remainder of the troops may safely unmask. It should be noted that bright light will cause contraction of the pupils which could be erroneously interpreted as a nerve agent symptom.

■ Procedures when no detector kit is available and when authorized:

- As an emergency field expedient when no detector kit can be obtained, two or three individuals are selected to take a deep breath, hold it, break the seal of their masks, and keep their eyes wide open for 15 seconds. They then clear their masks, reestablish the seal and wait for ten minutes. If no symptoms appear after ten minutes, the same individuals again break seal, take two or three breaths, and clear and reseal the mask. Wait another ten minutes, if no symptoms have developed, these same individuals unmask for five minutes and then remask. After ten more minutes, if no symptoms have appeared, the remainder of the group can safely unmask. However, they should all remain alert for the appearance of any chemical symptoms.

APPENDIX H

TACTICAL BIVOUACS

Duties of the Quartering Party

- Select a specific site prior to the arrival of the unit.
- Select definite areas within the bivouac site for each platoon.
- Conduct reconnaissance to determine security requirements.
- Mark unit areas and post necessary guides.
- Select head locations.

Duties of Leaders

- Establish security upon arrival:
  - Establish internal platoon security.
  - Establish outposts, as directed. Outposts should be organized at key points outside the bivouac site and be comprised of—
    - Crew-served weapons and personnel who man the key points.
    - One or two man sentinel posts to cover likely avenues of approach.
    - Patrols placed forward of sentinels.

Tactical Bivouacs   H-2

- If necessary, and when directed, establish forward security posts on key terrain beyond the limits of observation of sentinels.

■ Prescribe a definite area within the assigned area for each subordinate unit:

- Maintain tactical integrity.
- Provide sufficient area for dispersion.

■ Direct maximum use of cover and concealment.

■ Establish your own position from which positive control can be exercised.

■ Maintain the area in a proper state of police.

■ Inform subordinates of the location of the water point, mess area, head, and sickbay.

■ Ensure continuous combat readiness.

APPENDIX I

ARM AND HAND SIGNALS

DECREASE SPEED	
	Extend arm horizontally sidewards, palm to the front, and wave arm downward several times, keeping the arm straight. Arm does not move above the horizontal.

CHANGE DIRECTION OR COLUMN (RIGHT OR LEFT)	
	Extend arm horizontally to the side, palm to the front.

Arm and Hand Signals   I-2

ENEMY IN SIGHT	
	Hold the rifle horizontally, with the stock in the shoulder, the muzzle pointing in the direction of the enemy.

RANGE	
	Extend the arm fully toward the leader or men for whom the signal is intended with the fist closed. Open the fist exposing one finger for each 100 yards of range.

COMMENCE FIRING
Extend the arm in front of the body, hip high, palm down, and move it through a wide horizontal arc several times.

FIRE FASTER
Execute rapidly the signal **COMMENCE FIRING**. For machine guns, a change to the next higher rate of fire is prescribed.

Arm and Hand Signals

FORM COLUMN

Raise either arm to the vertical position. Drop the arm to the rear, describing complete circles in a vertical plane parallel to the body. The signal may be used to indicate either a troop or vehicular column.

ARE YOU READY?

Extend the arm toward the leader for whom the signal is intended, hand raised, fingers extended and joined, then raise arm slightly above horizontal, palm facing outward.

I AM READY	
	Execute the signal **ARE YOU READY?**

SHIFT	
	Raise the hand that is on the side toward the new direction across the body, palm to the front; then swing the arm in a horizontal arc, extending arm and hand to point in the new direction.

Arm and Hand Signals

Arm and Hand Signals   I-6

	ECHELON (RIGHT OR LEFT)
	Face the unit(s) being signaled and extend one arm 45° above and the other arm 45° below the horizontal, palms to the front. The lower arm indicates the direction of the echelon. Supplementary commands may be given to ensure prompt and proper execution.

	AS SKIRMISHERS (FIRE TEAM) LINE FORMATION (SQUAD)
	Raise both arms laterally until horizontal, arms and hands extended, palms down. If it is necessary to indicate a direction, move in the desired direction at the same time.

WEDGE	
	Extend both arms downward and to the sides at an angle of 45° below the horizontal, palms to the front.

VEE	
	Extend arms at an angle of 45° above the horizontal forming the letter "V" with arms and torso.

Arm and Hand Signals

FIRE TEAM	
	Place the right arm diagonally across the chest.

SQUAD	
	Extend the hand and arm toward the squad leader, palm of the hand down; distinctly move the hand up and down several times from the wrist, holding the arm steady.

PLATOON	
	Extend both arms forward, palms of the hands down, toward the leader(s) for whom the signal is intended. Describe large vertical circles with the hands.

CLOSE UP	
	Start signal with both arms extended sideward, palms up, and bring palms together overhead momentarily. When repetition of this signal is necessary, the arms are returned to the starting position by movement along the front of the body.

Arm and Hand Signals

Arm and Hand Signals

I-10

OPEN UP; EXTEND	
	Start signal with arms extended overhead, palms together, and bring arms to the horizontal position at the sides, palms down. When repetition of this signal is necessary the arms are returned along the front of the body to the starting position and the signal is repeated until understood.

DISPERSE	
	Extend either arm vertically overhead; wave the hand and arm to the front, left, right, and rear, the palm toward the direction of each movement.

ATTENTION	
	Extend the arm sidewards, slightly above horizontal, palm to the front; wave toward the head several times.

I DO NOT UNDERSTAND	
	Face toward the source of signal; raise both arms sidewards to the horizontal at hip level, bend both arms or elbows, palms up, and shrug shoulders in the manner of the universal "I dunno."

Arm and Hand Signals

I-12

FORWARD; ADVANCE; TO THE RIGHT, LEFT, OR REAR (USED WHEN STARTING FROM A HALT)	
	Face and move in the desired direction of march; at the same time extend the arm horizontally to the rear, then swing it overhead and forward in the direction of movement until it is horizontal, palm down.

HALT	
	Carry the hand to the shoulder, palm to the front; then thrust the hand upward vertically to the full extent of the arm and hold it in that position until the signal is understood.

DOWN; TAKE COVER	
	Extend arm sideward at an angle of 45° above horizontal, palm down, and lower it to side. Both arms may be used in giving this signal. Repeat until understood.

FREEZE	
	Make the signal for **HALT** and make a fist with the hand.

Arm and Hand Signals

INCREASE SPEED; DOUBLE TIME

Carry the hand to the shoulder, fist closed; rapidly thrust the fist upward vertically to the full extent of the arm and back to the shoulder several times. This signal is also used to increase gait or speed.

HASTY AMBUSH (RIGHT OR LEFT)

Raise fist to shoulder level and thrust it several times in the desired direction.

RALLY POINT	
	Touch the belt buckle with one hand and then point to the ground.

OBJECTIVE RALLY POINT	
	Touch the belt buckle with one hand, point to the ground, and make a circular motion with the hand.

HELICOPTER HANDLING SIGNALS

Day signals are indicated. Night signals are identical except for the addition of illuminated wands or other NVG compatible illumination.

WAVE-OFF	
	Arms rapidly waved and crossed over the head.

All of the following signals are considered a guide and do not require compliance by the pilot.

THIS WAY	
	Arms above head in vertical position with palms facing inward.

LANDING DIRECTION	
	Marshaler stands with arms raised vertically above head and facing toward the point where the aircraft is to land. The arms are lowered repeatedly from a vertical to a horizontal position, stopping finally in the horizontal position.

Arm and Hand Signals

I-18

STOP	
	Arms crossed above the head, palms facing forward.

HOVER	
	Arms extended horizontally sideways, palms downward.

MOVE TO RIGHT	
	Left arm extended horizontally sideways in direction of movement and other arm swung over the head in same direction, in a repeating movement.

MOVE TO LEFT	
	Right arm extended horizontally sideways in direction of movement and other arm swung over the head in same direction, in a repeating movement.

Arm and Hand Signals　　　　　　　　　　　　　　　　　　　I-20

MOVE AHEAD	
	Arms shoulder width apart, palms facing backwards and repeatedly moved upward-backward from shoulder height.

MOVE BACK	
	Arms by sides, palms facing forward, swept forward and upward repeatedly to shoulder height.

MOVE UPWARD	
	Arms extended horizontally sideways beckoning upwards, with palms turned up. Speed of movement indicates rate of ascent.

MOVE DOWNWARD	
	Arms extended horizontally sideways beckoning downwards, with palms turned down. Speed of movement indicates the rate of descent.

Arm and Hand Signals

LAND	
	Arms crossed and extended downwards in front of the body.

TURN TO LEFT	
	Point right arm downward, left arm is repeatedly moved upward-backward. Speed of arm movement indicates the rate of turn.

TURN TO RIGHT	
	Point left arm downward, right hand repeatedly moved upward-backward. Speed of arm movement indicates rate of turn.

TAKEOFF	
	Conceal left hand and make circular motion of right hand over the head in horizontal plane ending in a throwing motion of arm towards direction of takeoff.

Arm and Hand Signals

I-24

AFFIRMATIVE (ALL CLEAR)	
	Hand raised, thumb up.

NEGATIVE (NOT CLEAR)	
	Arm held out, hand below waist level, thumb turned downwards.

CLEARANCE FOR PERSONNEL TO APPROACH AIRCRAFT	
	A beckoning motion with right hand at eye level.

PERSONNEL APPROACHING THE AIRCRAFT	
	Left hand raised vertically overhead, palm towards aircraft. The other hand indicates to personnel concerned and gestures towards aircraft.

Arm and Hand Signals   I-25

Arm and Hand Signals I-26

	RELEASE LOAD
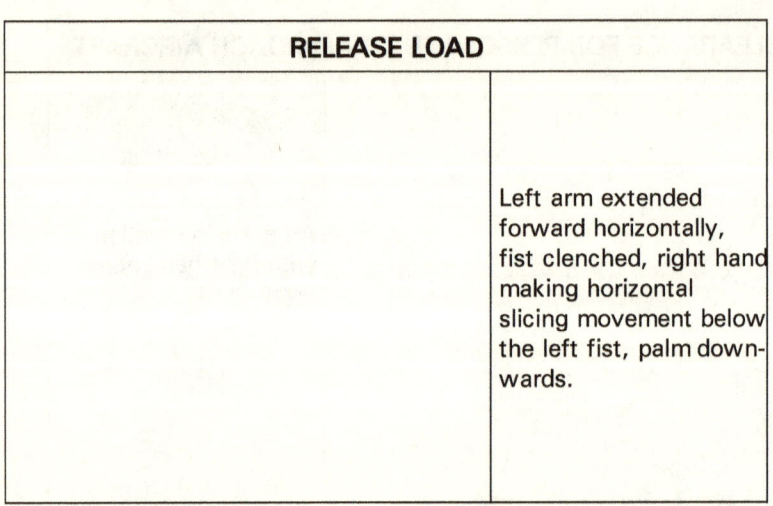	Left arm extended forward horizontally, fist clenched, right hand making horizontal slicing movement below the left fist, palm downwards.

	LOAD HAS NOT BEEN RELEASED
	Bend left arm horizontally across chest with fist clenched, palm downward; open right hand pointed up vertically to center of left fist.

HOOK UP LOAD	
	Rope climbing motion with hands.

WINCH DOWN	
	Left arm horizontal in front of body, fist clenched, right hand with palm turned downwards making downward motion.

Arm and Hand Signals

Arm and Hand Signals

WINCH UP	
	Left arm horizontal in front of body, fist clenched, right hand with palm turned upwards making upward motion.

CUT CABLE	
	A signal similar to **RELEASE LOAD** except that the right hand has the palm downward and not clenched. Rapid repetition of right hand movement indicates urgency.

ARM AND HAND SIGNALS FOR MECHANIZED INFANTRY

HALT

DECREASE SPEED

Arm and Hand Signals

I-30

LEFT TURN OR COLUMN LEFT	RIGHT TURN OR COLUMN RIGHT
Turn in direction the arm is pointing.	Turn in direction the arm is pointing.

OPEN UP	CLOSE UP
Extend distance between men or vehicles	Decrease distance between men or

DIAMOND/COIL FORMATION	COLUMN FORMATION

WEDGE FORMATION	ECHELON LEFT

Arm and Hand Signals

I-32

ECHELON RIGHT	LINE FORMATION

START ENGINES	STOP ENGINES

MOUNT	DISMOUNT

MOVE IN REVERSE	CHANGE DIRECTION
	Turn in direction of closed fist.

Arm and Hand Signals

I-34

NEUTRAL STEER	CLOSE UP DISTANCE BETWEEN VEHICLES AND

PASS AND KEEP GOING	CONTACT RIGHT (LEFT)

| ATTENTION | TAKE UP FIRE POSITION |

| ACKNOWLEDGED | I DO NOT UNDERSTAND |

Arm and Hand Signals

Arm and Hand Signals

I-36

AS YOU WERE OR DISREGARD PREVIOUS CMD	BUTTON-UP OR UNBUTTON

AIR ATTACK	ASSEMBLY OR RALLY

| TRAVELING | BOUNDING OVERWATCH |

| TRAVELING OVERWATCH | VEE FORMATION |

Arm and Hand Signals I-38

HERRINGBONE FORMATION	ACTION LEFT (RIGHT)

RAMP UP AND DOGGED (Day)	RAMP UP AND DOGGED (Night)

RAMP DOWN (Day)	RAMP DOWN (Night)

Arm and Hand Signals
I-40

NIGHT VISUAL SIGNALS FOR MECHANIZED INFANTRY

START ENGINES	STOP VEHICLE OR ENGINES

TURN LEFT	TURN RIGHT

GO FORWARD; MOVE OUT; INCREASE SPEED	MOVE IN REVERSE
	Light is blinking.

Arm and Hand Signals

Arm and Hand Signals   I-42

FLAG SIGNALS FOR MECHANIZED INFANTRY AND TANKS

MOUNT

DISMOUNT

DISMOUNT AND ASSAULT

Arm and Hand Signals

Arm and Hand Signals I-44

ASSEMBLE OR CLOSE

MOVE OUT

NBC HAZARD PRESENT

DANGER OR ENEMY IN SIGHT

Arm and Hand Signals I-46

ALL CLEAR; READY; OR UNDERSTOOD

DISREGARD OR VEHICLE OUT OF ACTION

LIVE FIRE RANGE FLAGS

Green	Red
GUNS ELEVATED	
Green and Yellow	**Red and Yellow**
MALFUNCTION	MALFUNCTION WEAPONS LOADED
Yellow	**Red and Green**
	CONDUCTING 1. PREPARE-TO-FIRE EXERCISES 2. NONFIRING EXERCISES

Arm and Hand Signals

Arm and Hand Signals   I-48

Yellow

Yellow   Red   Green

Yellow   Red   Green

Yellow   Red   Green

Yellow   Red   Green

Yellow   Red   Green

Yellow   Red   Green

Yellow   Red   Green

Yellow   Red   Green

Yellow   Red   Green

Yellow   Red   Green

APPENDIX J

GLOSSARY

AAV .... assault amphibious vehicle
APICM .... anti-personnel improved conventional munitions

BOMBREP .... bomb report

CAS .... close air support
CP .... command post
CRRC .... combat rubber raiding craft
CVT .... controlled variable time

DASC .... direct air support center
DPICM .... dual-purpose improved conventional munitions
DRAW-D .... defend; reinforce; attack; withdraw; delay

EPW .... enemy prisoner of war

FDC .... fire direction center
FEBA .... forward edge of the battle area
FO .... forward observer
FPF .... final protective fire
FPL .... final protective line
FSCC .... fire support coordination center

HE .... high explosive
HRST .... helicopter rope suspension training

Glossary J-1

Glossary

IP .... initial point

JTAR .... joint tactical air request

LAV .... light armored vehicle
LD .... line of departure
LP .... listening post

METT-T .... mission, enemy, terrain and weather, troops and support available-time available
MOPP .... mission-oriented protective posture
MORTREP .... mortar report

NBC .... nuclear, biological, and chemical
NEO .... noncombatant evacuation operation

OCOKA .... observation and fields of fire, cover and concealment, obstacles, key terrain, and avenues of approach
OP .... observation post
ORP .... objective rally point

PDF .... principal direction of fire
PLD .... probable line of deployment
POL .... petroleum, oils, and lubricants

Q .... fuze quick

RED .... record of emergency data
ROE .... rules of engagement
RRC .... rigid raiding craft

SALUTE	size, activity, location, unit, time, equipment
SHELREP	shelling report
SMAW	shoulder-launched multipurpose assault weapon
SP	sentinel post
SPIE	special patrol insertion and extraction
VT	variable time
WP	white phosphorus

www.ingramcontent.com/pod-product-compliance
Lightning Source LLC
Chambersburg PA
CBHW022101150426
43195CB00008B/217